—THE—
RESILIENCY
TOOLKIT

*A Busy Parent's Guide to Raising
Happy, Confident, Successful Children*

CALVERT F CAZIER, PHD, MPH &
ANNE EVANS-CAZIER, LCSW

Publishing Services provided by Paper Raven Books

Printed in the United States of America

First Printing, 2019

Paperback ISBN= 978-1-7337882-0-5
Hardback ISBN= 978-1-7337882-1-2

WHAT PEOPLE ARE SAYING

"You don't need to change everything about yourself or your child to enjoy the rewards of a stronger family. I wish this book had been available earlier. Clients I see today would have benefitted from having parents who used the loving skills described in this very valuable book."
— *Ellyn Bader, PhD, Co-founder of The Couples Institute*

"With just a few minutes a day, you will find the inspiration and practical strategies you need to guide your child along the path to happiness, well-being, and success."
— *Mrs. Jeanette Herbert, First Lady of Utah*

"What a delightful read. Even though the authors are well-educated experts, they also provide priceless counsel in a friendly, easy-to-read, practical, universally applicable, 'sit around the table and chat' format."
— *Glenn E. Richardson, PhD, Professor, College of Health, University of Utah, Author of Proactive and Applied Resilience: The Sixteen Experiences*

"A 'must-read' for any parent wishing to help build a resilient family and help their children face the unique challenges of life in the 21st century. This book is a wonderful guide full of useful strategies for doing just that!"
— *Carl Hanson, PhD, Department Chair, College of Health, Brigham Young University*

DEDICATED TO OUR FAMILY

Paul & Lois Cazier and David & Joy Evans, our parents, who loved us, taught us, laughed with us, cried with us, put up with us, and most importantly inspired us.

Our children, Paul and Jenny, Laurel and Christopher, Ally and Tony, Peter, Michelle and Marshall, who have also loved us, taught us, helped us find our way, laughed with us, cried with us, definitely put up with us, and inspired us.

Our grandchildren, Calvert & Camille, Samantha, Jocelyn, Edwin, Matthew, Jackson, Hyrum, Alicia, Lydia, and Joshua, and our great-granddaughter, Rebecca, who continue to love us, teach us, help us stretch, grow, laugh, and cry, and who keep on putting up with us as we fail forward together.

Thank you, we are most fortunate to be family.

TABLE OF CONTENTS

Chapter 4: Forgiveness 53

*Like all of us, your child has been hurt and will be
again. She needs empathy for others and the ability to
forgive in order to move forward.*

Chapter 5: Self-Worth 77

*A sense of personal worth underpins your child's
confidence in his ability to face life resiliently and do the
work necessary to move forward towards his dreams.*

Chapter 6: Humor 97

*Being able to see the humor in life will help your child
take the inevitable bumps and bruises less personally and
be more flexible in how she sees herself and others.*

Chapter 7: Family Traditions

Strong yet flexible family traditions ground your child through sorrow and joy and root her growing sense of self to the past and the future.

Chapter 8: Wisdom

Your child needs you to help him develop the wisdom essential to making good choices about his current and future life.

Chapter 9: Values   155

*Through shared experiences, you can guide your child
as she seeks out and defines her own values and the
principles that will guide her life choices.*

Chapter 10: Hope and Optimism   175

*A belief in the future and a sense that effort will be
worthwhile are key to your child's contentment in the
here and now and his motivation to keep working and
moving forward.*

Chapter 11: Dreams and Goals 199

*Having a vision of the future and effective ways of
working towards those dreams give purpose, meaning,
and direction to your child's efforts.*

Chapter 12: Hard Work 219

*The ability to apply himself, persevere, and keep working
are vital to your child successfully pursuing his dreams
and goals.*

A sense of something greater than herself opens up your child's life, her maturing sense of the universe, and her place in it.

You and your child are enjoying greater resiliency and are ready to take on today and the future with more confidence and success.

Worksheets to go along with the skills taught in Chapter 2: The Toolkit Begins Here.

Chapter 1

ESSENTIAL GUIDE: HOW TO GET THE MOST OUT OF THIS BOOK

"Would you like me to give you a formula for success? It's quite simple, really. Double your rate of failure. You are thinking of failure as the enemy of success. But it isn't at all. You can be discouraged by failure, or you can learn from it. So go ahead and make mistakes. Make all you can. Because remember, that's where you will find success."
Thomas Watson, former chairman and CEO of IBM

As a parent today, you are busy, stretched thin. There's too much to do and not enough time. You want the best for your child but wonder how to do it all.

Like most parents, you probably have both hopes and fears for your child. Maybe you worry that your child argues too much, spends too much time on her phone, doesn't do his chores, doesn't do her homework, is getting bullied at school, is being a bully at school, doesn't have friends, doesn't have the right kind of friends—the list goes on.

You also hope your child will be happy, confident, and successful. It doesn't matter if your child is starting daycare or going away to college; as a parent, you want him to be learning, growing, overcoming challenges, and moving forward. In other words, you want your child to be resilient.

No matter the age of your child, you want to share a good relationship. Yet, in every relationship, people make mistakes, do things they wish they hadn't, or fail to do things they wish they had. Now is the time to profit from mistakes, repair the hurts and pains of life, practice forgiving self and others, become better parents, and move forward. It's time to become more resilient.

Yes, you are busy and there is a lot to do, but it doesn't have to be overwhelming. In just a few minutes a day, you can take small steps that will add up and make a big difference. You don't need to read this whole book all at once. Take it in little chunks. Choose one thing, stick with it for a while, and then come back again when you are ready.

Pick a chapter that seems important to your family right now. You will find practical strategies to adapt and use across a broad range of ages and problems. Not knowing each family's situation, we chose to switch back and forth, using both male and female pronouns.

We included stories to encourage flexible, creative thought and inspire you to broaden your vision of the possible. Stories have long been recognized as powerful mediums of lasting change. They are fun to read and stick in the mind long after the book is closed.

People have been telling stories since they first gathered around the fire at night. Recent research highlights the benefits of storytelling. Stories can:

- Stimulate us to action
- Open our minds to different ways of thinking
- Inspire us to see life from multiple perspectives
- Motivate us to accept and use new information in our lives
- Help us recognize and understand both similarities and differences between ourselves and others to develop bonds of trust, friendship, and support
- Teach important life lessons to our children

In this book, you will find the insight and guidance you need to help your child face the challenges of today, and the future, with greater resiliency. You don't need to change everything about yourself, or your child, or your parenting overnight. A little effort here, a few minutes there, and suddenly, your resiliency skills will strengthen, your relationships will change, and your family will be stronger.

Our Story

You might like to know a little more about us and why we are so passionate about helping parents raise more resilient children. We bring a unique and powerful combination of experiences and strengths to this work.

Cal: I love telling stories and draw on a lifetime of working to overcome the challenges of Tourette syndrome as well as obsessive-compulsive disorder (OCD) and attention deficit disorder (ADD). In spite of being told I really wasn't college material, I somehow managed not only to graduate college but to also go on to complete a master's degree and PhD in public health. My stories come from the pains and joys of raising two sons, my personal struggles developing my own resiliency, stories I heard from my parents and grandparents, my experience as a college professor for over 30 years, my long career in public health motivating people to lead safer, healthier lives, and, of course, my own active imagination!

Anne: I've been in a lot of homes with a lot of families throughout my career as a mental health professional, from Head Start preschoolers to low income seniors. One of my favorite careers was being a stay-at-home mom with my three daughters. Mind you, that doesn't mean that every minute was joyful and fulfilling. There were plenty of moments of sheer boredom, tedious chores, tears and clenched fists, but, for me, these were worth the other moments of laughter, sweet smiles, and shared adventures. After the girls grew up, I went to graduate school and became a licensed clinical social worker. Since 1999, I have been a therapist helping people heal their lives and their relationships. I keep a quote from Maya Angelou in my office where I can see it at all times, "I did what I knew best, and when I knew better, I did better." That sums up my greatest belief that we can learn from our experiences and move forward.

Cal and Anne: We have five kids, ten grandkids, and our very first great-granddaughter! We've come through multiple bouts of cancer, infertility, the death of a spouse and a grandchild, divorce, combining two families into a blended one, and so much more. What really excites us is helping parents answer the question, "How can I help my child be more successful today, tomorrow, the next day, and the next?"

What Is Resiliency Anyway?

"I have not failed. I've just found 10,000 ways that won't work."
Thomas Edison

Resiliency is not something that you either have or don't have or that only a few special people can have. Each of us can become more resilient. It is never too early or too late to start building it.

Very simply stated, resiliency is the ability to face challenges, get knocked down by them, and use the experience to grow stronger and move forward. Some people call this "failing forward." Undoubtedly, you are familiar with stories of Thomas Edison's tinkering in his lab and his innumerable creative "failures." You also know about his astounding creations: the light bulb, the phonograph, and motion pictures, to name a few. His life is a major testament to the power of resiliency, to the value of learning from your experiences and seeing big and little setbacks and obstacles as opportunities to learn, try something new, and move forward.

There are different ways to think of resiliency. It can be viewed as a concept, an idea; as a mindset, a set of assumptions and attitudes that impact how a person thinks and acts; or as a skill, the ability to do something well as a result of training and experience. All of these views have merit, but we have chosen the latter. We see resiliency as a skill that can be acquired by gaining knowledge and practice. It can be broken down into subsets of skills, and mastery of each of those skills contributes to overall resiliency. We can all become more masterful through deliberate, sustained effort to learn and apply our growing knowledge more and more skillfully.

Research on resiliency has exploded in recent years. Researchers have identified numerous skills highly associated with resiliency and have explored how those skills can be developed. From these, we selected 11 key areas and devoted a chapter to each one. Growth in each of these areas will also help your child create stronger, healthier relationships with you and others, a vital foundation for lifelong resiliency.

Becoming skillful at anything takes practice, and resiliency is no exception. When we begin to practice something new and unfamiliar, it is likely to be difficult at first, and there is always a risk that it will be harder than we thought it would be. We might miscalculate, stumble, fall, and even have a few miserable failures. Why would we risk that? What benefits would be worth taking such a chance? As one of our resiliency heroes, Nelson Mandela, said, "The greatest glory in living lies not in never falling, but in rising every time we fall."

Part of being resilient is realizing that none of us ever really knows where we are in the big picture of life. Moments that feel like failure right now may turn out to be positive turning points or stepping-stones in a much larger process. In the middle of what feels like a disaster, we may be learning valuable lessons that will serve us now and in the future. We help our children gain this perspective as we model trying, stumbling, making adjustments, and trying again. We can let children know that we expect them to fail once in a while. If they're not ever stumbling or struggling, they may be playing it too safe, avoiding healthy challenges, and limiting their growth. One of the keys to long-term resiliency is to remain curious about what might come next.

When Cal was in high school, he had one of those moments that, at the time, could easily have been seen as a "failure," but which, in fact, turned out to be one of the most important positive turning points of his life.

So What?: A Lesson in Resiliency

"You may encounter many defeats, but you must not be defeated."
Dr. Maya Angelou

Through high school, I was at best an average student. I earned mostly Cs, some Bs, a few Ds, and occasionally an A. I remember that I took an aptitude test to determine what I might be capable of doing after high school. When the results came back, I was called into the counselor's office to discuss my future.

I sat uncomfortably across the desk from the counselor, who seemed to stare at me. He asked, "What do you want to do after you graduate?"

I responded, "I don't know exactly what I want, but I know I want to go to college."

At this point, the counselor proceeded to explain the facts about being a college student. "For every hour of class average students take, they can expect two hours of homework. So if they take the average load of 15 hours, then they will be spending approximately 30 hours per week doing homework, or 45 hours of schoolwork all together."

He went on to explain that my scores on the aptitude test were so low that if I went to college, I would need to spend four hours doing homework for every hour I was in class. "Therefore," he said, "you will need to spend 60 hours per week doing homework, plus the 15 hours in the classroom, for a total of 75 hours each week."

Now I have always had good hand/eye coordination, and one part of the test required stacking washers on wooden pegs. I did very well on this part. Based on his perception of my future struggles in college and my scores on "washer stacking," the counselor recommended that I capitalize on my great manual dexterity, go to trade school, and pursue a career as a typesetter.

I left that room believing that he had told me that I wasn't smart enough or capable enough to go to college. Perhaps he didn't say that exactly, but I am certain to this day that that is what he meant. I was devastated.

When I got home that day, the first person I saw was my mother. She could tell that something was bothering me, and even though I tried denying it, she was gently persistent, as a good mother should be. Eventually, I broke down and told her about my experience with the counselor. When I got through telling her what happened, she looked me in the eyes and said two words to me: "So what?"

She elaborated, "So what if you have to study harder than others? That man doesn't know your desire. So what if you have to work harder? That man doesn't know anything about your work ethic. So what if school is hard for you? That man doesn't know anything about your talents and hidden abilities." She went on to help me understand that if I wanted a college education badly enough, that man holding my test scores couldn't stop me.

That day, my mother motivated me and helped me understand that if I wanted a college education, then it was up to me. She planted seeds of self-esteem and belief in myself. She helped me become more resilient, which I surely needed to get through college!

I went on to college and graduated with a BS degree, a master of public health degree, and finally a PhD. In hindsight, I realize that this little teaching moment with my mom, when my future looked bleak and I felt like such a failure, was one of those major turning points in my life. This moment, along with many other moments, helped me develop the resiliency to push through the challenges I've had to face. I've come to understand that resilience is something we can learn, and it is available to all who are willing to pay the price of developing it.

I have told and retold this story many times to help my children, grandchildren, and others accept their challenges, grow stronger, and never give up on themselves. You may use this story, or any of the stories in this book with your family, and we hope you begin to tell your own stories about your life and your family. As you do, you strengthen your family bonds and foster resiliency.

A Better Way

"It's not the load that breaks you down. It's the way you carry it."
C. S. Lewis

In our work, we hear a lot about the challenges families struggle with today. Some of them you pretty much have to expect in every family: whining, complaining, arguing, fighting, playing too many video games, spending too much time on social media, or hitting puberty. Others are ultimate challenges: death, divorce, integrating new family members, sexually transmitted diseases, addictions, or suicidal thoughts. It can be overwhelming to think about dealing with even a single one of these challenges, and yet, realistically, you can expect to face a great number of challenges both big and small as your child grows up. Many parents wear themselves out running from one problem to the next, chasing solutions for each one.

We present a better way of responding to challenges that is simple, powerful, and effective: *build resilience*. Being a resilient parent means providing a foundation for your child to learn how to face challenges, assess options more clearly and creatively, grow stronger from overcoming a challenge, and be better prepared to build a healthy future.

We believe that being a parent is the most important job there is. It's probably the most difficult as well. Children need parents to guide and support them along the way to becoming more resilient.

There Is a Tricky (And Exciting) Part...

To help our children become more resilient, most of us need to build our own resilience as well. The good news is that you and your child can grow alongside each other, become more resilient, push yourselves to experiment with new things, think of setbacks and failures as friends and teachers, open yourselves up to new perspectives and creative solutions, and always get back up and move forward again.

Hope, Possibility, and Choice

"Every day brings new choices."
Martha Beck

You can feel hopeful, even if your current family relationships are far from ideal. This book contains the inspiration and practical strategies to help you, your child, and your relationship grow stronger and more resilient. Resiliency grows step-by-step, woven into daily life. It needs to be lived. It can't be learned on a purely academic level. So, as you help your child become more resilient, you will inevitably find yourself stretching and growing alongside her.

Each family faces a unique set of challenges. Here are a few big picture examples of how you might apply this book to a specific family situation. Effectively facing whatever challenges your child has right now will help her grow stronger, wiser, and better prepared to face whatever comes in the unknown and unknowable future. This is what building resiliency is all about.

Bullying

There have always been bullies, but because of the ubiquitous presence of cell phones, internet, and social media, bullying today has new dimensions that can make it more brutal and devastating than ever before. Perhaps a group of kids at school are making unwanted, inappropriate sexual comments to a teenage girl, spreading rumors about her, and taunting her online. Maybe a young boy in grade school is repeatedly teased, called names, or left out. Cell phones today can quickly send damaging pictures and hurtful texts to a whole lot of people all at once. Fear and pain escalate rapidly. Think about how developing each of the following resiliency skills could strengthen these children's ability to face such painful challenges:

- a strong sense of self-worth,
- an ability to maintain hope and optimism in the face of adversity,
- an established pattern of being able to give and receive forgiveness while protecting themselves from further harm, and
- a great sense of humor that enables them to take things less personally and be more flexible in their thinking.

Screen Time

There are so many devices with countless apps available today that it often feels like our children are loose in a virtual candy store. They have endless tempting and exciting ways to spend life glued to a screen, from Facebook, Twitter, Snapchat, Instagram, texting, online gaming, and pornography, to who knows what next? Again, imagine how developing each of the following resiliency skills could help children navigate their choices:

- a clearly thought-out set of deeply held personal values,
- a strong, supportive network of healthy relationships with family and friends of many ages,
- powerful traditions that bind the family together across the generations, and
- deeply rooted spiritual connections to something bigger than themselves.

Homework

The bane of existence in many a home, homework can feel like a constant battle. Questions like, Do you have any? Have you done it? Did you turn it in? may seem to be a recurring theme in your life. Consider how developing each of the following resiliency skills could help turn homework into a more positive learning experience:

- well thought-out dreams and goals,
- deeply engrained habits of hard work,
- and a sense of gratitude for the opportunities of life, including knowledge, growth, and education.

Are You Ready?

Think about your child's strengths and challenges right now. Take a few minutes to read through the table of contents and the 11 resiliency skills covered in this book. Reflect on your philosophy of parenting and how developing these skills could help your child. Which resiliency skills do you think would be most helpful right now?

Think about the long term. Consider each of the resiliency skills and how developing each of them would prepare your child to face future challenges. Think of your own values and which of the resiliency skills are therefore high on your list of priorities to encourage in your child.

Your best-laid plans won't always turn out exactly how you hope they will, but rising when you fall is what counts. This applies not only to your child's efforts, but to your own parenting efforts as well. Your child is going to have a ringside seat to your new ways of parenting, some of which will work out great and some of which will fall short. Perhaps most importantly of all, your child will watch and learn as you adjust, get creative, try something different, and try again and again and again. You will be teaching resiliency in the most powerful way possible—by example.

Need more help? We are here to support you all the way. We want to hear about your victories, challenges, and questions. Contact us at www.ResilientChild.com

Let's Get Started!

"The secret of getting ahead is getting started."
Mark Twain

Are you excited and ready to jump into a chapter that caught your interest? Before you dive into any other chapters, we strongly encourage you to first read Chapter 2: The Toolkit Begins Here, where you will learn how to set successful goals, communicate more effectively with your child, and help everyone stay calm through the process. After reading that chapter, please feel free to read chapters in any order that resonates with you and start adding more resiliency skills to your toolkit. We hope you enjoy the journey, feel inspired, apply what you learn, and work hard to develop your child's resiliency and your own.

Here's to failing forward!

Chapter 2

THE TOOLKIT BEGINS HERE

*"Enjoy the little things, for one day you may look back
and realize they were the big things."*
Robert Brault

With any job, it helps to have the right tools. Parenting is no exception. Would you change a tire without a jack, or do the laundry without detergent? Lots of parents take on vital parenting tasks without the basic tools for success. Three critical tools are the ability to:

1. **Set goals** to turn dreams into reality,
2. **Communicate clearly** with your child along the way, and
3. **Stay emotionally grounded** when the pressure is on.

Tool #1: Setting Successful Goals

"It's not only children who grow. Parents do, too. As much as we watch to see what our children do with their lives, they are watching us to see what we do with ours. I can't tell my children to reach for the sun. All I can do is reach for it myself."
Joyce Maynard

As a parent who wants to raise a more resilient child, you face a dilemma. Hopefully, you are beginning to see how much your child would benefit from developing resiliency skills, yet your child himself probably doesn't have the same vision. No doubt what you want for him is in his best interests, yet likely he does not have your same wisdom and insight. You will need to keep this in mind as you plan for your child's future.

To turn dreams into reality, you need to set goals, which will serve as action steps to take you in a desired direction. Since this direction is desired by you—and not necessarily by your child— you need to set goals for yourself, not for your child. Your goals will outline the steps *you* can take to guide and support your child and encourage her to grow and develop in the direction of your dreams, the value of which she is unlikely to grasp right now.

Let's look at an example. Many parents tell Anne that one of their biggest problems is that their school-age children are disrespectful. They don't come when called, don't do their chores when asked, talk back, whine and fuss, and don't want to do things with the family. These parents have a dream that their children will be more respectful, more involved, and more appreciative of family life. This may actually be very much in their children's best interests in the bigger picture of life, but at this moment, it is probably the parents' dream and *not* the children's dream. Does this distinction make sense now?

If you try to set goals for your child, you will likely face lots of resistance and little success. Instead, set goals for yourself. Set goals to change the way you interact with your child, action steps you can take that will help you foster your child's growth and support his developing resiliency in the face of life's challenges. In every section of this book, you will find practical strategies that support this kind of effective action and will help you make your dreams become reality.

And, of course, there's just this little catch…

When we aspire to something new or better, there is always a catch. There is one part of us that gets excited, pumped up, ready to go, AND there is another part of us that says, "Umm, yes, sounds good, BUT…" A part of us wants to move forward with change, and another part of us wants to hold back, worried that we might fall short or fail, so maybe it would be better if we don't try. Sound familiar?

Of course it sounds familiar. It happens to all of us. It happens to you. It happens to your child. It happens to anyone who tries to stretch for a new goal.

Is there even a part of you that would like to know what to do about it? If so, we invite you to experiment with the following seven-step exercise. When you become comfortable with it, you can teach it to your child.

Moving from "Yes, But" to "Yes, And"

To get started, make a copy of the Setting Successful Goals worksheet found in the appendix and get a pen or pencil, or download the worksheet onto your laptop or tablet. Please start with a hard copy instead of one on your desktop computer because you will need to move your location during the exercise. (This is important and will be explained in more detail as you read along.)

Step one. Choose a comfortable place to sit, take a couple of relaxing breaths, and then focus on the part of you that wants to make a change. Identify a broad, big picture of the change you would like to see.

Here's an example:

1. **A big picture change I would like to see is:** I'd like my child to be more respectful.

Uh oh, watch out. Remember, this kind of dream is likely your dream, and not a dream your child shares right now, even though it may be a great idea and would be in her best interest. With this in mind, be careful with the kinds of goals you set in step two.

Step two. Once you have in mind a clear idea of the overarching, big-picture change you want, break it down into specific action items to work on, small goals to take you in the direction of the change you desire. You can list as many small goals as you want. Then pick one to start working on, and put a check mark in front of it.

Here's an example of how tempting it is to make a list of goals for your child instead of yourself:

2. **Small goals in the desired direction:**

   a. My child will come promptly to the table for dinner when called.
   b. My child will pick up his belongings and put them away.

These are reasonable expectations and good things for your child to do, but they are goals for him, not goals for you. This is your dream, so set goals for yourself to help and support your child as he stretches and grows. Let's try again.

   a. I will teach my child how to help me prepare dinner. We will work together for the last 20 minutes before dinner is ready. I will do my best to be respectful and have fun while we work together.

b. I will work alongside my child and instruct him in age-appropriate expectations for putting his belongings away. I will make sure he knows what I expect and how to do it. I will find ways to have fun and enjoy the time we spend working together.

Step three. Take a couple of relaxing breaths and ask the part of you that wants to make a change, "What would be the benefits of the change I have in mind?" Start writing out a list of all of the benefits you can imagine might be possible if you choose to stretch and move in your desired direction. List as many as you can think of, the big ones and the little ones. Push yourself to make as complete a list as you can and to actually write it down. This will make it more powerful—powerful enough to help you really reach your goals.

Here's an example:

3. **The benefits of this change would be:**

For example, your initial list might be:

a. I would be less frustrated.
b. Dinner would start off more pleasantly.
c. I would feel more respected and appreciated.
d. I would be less likely to start yelling at my child.
e. We might all have a better time, talk more, and have more fun if dinner started off without having to drag him to the table.

Now review your list of benefits and rewrite as needed to make sure you focus in a positive way on what you want, rather than on what you don't want:

a. I would be more calm and relaxed.
b. Dinner would start off more pleasantly.
c. I would feel more respected and appreciated.
d. I would be more likely to speak to my child in a kind and respectful manner.
e. We might all have a better time, talk more, and have more fun if dinner started off **on a good note.**

Step four. Get up out of that nice, comfortable chair you are all settled into, take your writing materials, move to another place, and sit down there. You are probably tempted to ignore this direction and think, "Oh, that's silly, I'll just stay here." If there is even a little part of you that seriously wants to make some changes in your family, please consider experimenting with all the steps of this exercise. Once you move to the second spot, take a couple more relaxing breaths, and then focus on the part of you that says, "Yes, that change sounds nice, BUT…"

This is the part of you that has a list of reasons why change will be too hard, won't be worth it, won't work, won't last, etc. Allow yourself to really listen to this part of you for a few minutes. Value this part of you just as much as you value the part that wants something better. If you ignore this part of you, you undermine your chances for being successful in making the changes you want and bringing about the benefits you and your family deserve.

Write down everything you can think of that might get in your way as you work on making positive changes. Be as thorough and honest with yourself as you can. Write down your thoughts, even if they seem silly, trivial, or embarrassing. How would change be hard for you? Do you doubt your child will listen to you or give you a chance? Are you skeptical because you have gotten excited before and tried to make changes, but they didn't work? Or they worked for a while and then fizzled? Do you feel discouraged, overwhelmed, hopeless, or afraid your family just can't or won't change?

Just like the list of benefits, push yourself to make this list as complete as possible, and to actually write it down. This list of "BUTS" is just as important as the list of benefits.

Here's an example:

4. I want to make a change, BUT...

    a. He never listens to a thing I say.
    b. He is glued to his phone and video games.
    c. I've tried a million different ways to get his attention. Nothing works.
    d. It will just start another fight.
    e. Why should I have to do all this work? He should just come when he's called.

Review your list and include an emotion to go with each of your thoughts. Search deep to find and label your emotions. There is always at least one emotion connected with each of these powerful "BUTS."

    a. I'm **hurt and angry** that he never listens to a thing I say.
    b. I'm **frustrated** that he is glued to his phone and video games.
    c. I feel **hopeless** after trying a million different ways to get his attention. I'm **afraid** that nothing will ever work.
    d. I **fear** it will just start another fight.
    e. I'm **frazzled and overwhelmed**. Why should I have to do all this work? He should just come when he's called.

Step five. Go back, read over your list of benefits in Step three, and pick the three that really mean the most to you personally. Sometimes, you might realize that one or two of the benefits naturally go together, and you can combine them. Put a little check mark by the most important. Then look over your list of "BUTS" and pick the three from that list that are the most significant for you right now. Put a little check mark by them.

Here is an example:

5. **Benefits:**

   a. I would be more calm and relaxed.
   b. Dinner would start off more pleasantly.
   c. I would feel more respected and appreciated.
   d. I would be more likely to speak to my child in a kind and respectful manner.
   e. We might all have a better time, talk more, and have more fun, if dinner started off on a good note.

   Buts:

   a. I'm hurt and angry that he never listens to a thing I say.
   b. I'm frustrated that he is glued to his phone and video games.
   c. I'm feeling hopeless after trying a million different ways to get his attention. I'm afraid that nothing will ever work.
   d. I fear it will just start another fight.
   e. I'm frazzled and overwhelmed. Why should I have to do all this work? He should just come when he's called.

Step six. Fill in the following script:

Even though (write in the first "BUT" from the three you checked);

Even though (write in the second "BUT" from the three you checked);

Even though (write in the third "BUT" from the three you checked);

There is a part of me that wants and believes that I/we can (write in the first benefit from the three you checked);

There is a part of me that wants and believes that I/we can (write in the second benefit from the three you checked);

There is a part of me that wants and believes that I/we can (write in the third benefit from the three you checked).

Here's an example:

6. Write out the following script, filling in the blanks:

Even though I'm feeling hopeless after trying a million different ways to get his attention, and I'm afraid that nothing will ever work;
Even though I fear it will just start another fight;
Even though I'm frustrated that my child is glued to his phone and video games;
There is a part of me that wants and believes that I can speak in a kind and respectful manner to my child, and in turn be more respected and appreciated;
There is a part of me that wants and believes that I can be more calm and relaxed;

There is a part of me that wants and believes that <u>my family can have a better time, talk more, and have more fun during dinner.</u>

Step seven. Read your script out loud. When you finish reading it out loud, ask yourself this question: "How am I beginning to feel?" Make note of your answer and how you are beginning to feel in this moment. Pay attention to the intensity of your emotions, where you are experiencing any physical sensations in your body (like tension in your neck, pressure in your chest, a queasy feeling in your gut, a lump in your throat). Note the type and intensity of these sensations and what they might be trying to tell you.

Once you have your script completed, you are ready for action!

Choose a goal and get started.

⸎ Repeat this process regularly as you work on stretching towards your goals for change and growth. Fine-tune your script as you make progress or when you run into new or unexpected challenges.

We hope you will experiment with this exercise. It is one way you and your family can move from, "Yes, but" to "Yes, and." The "Yes" is the dream, the aspiration; the "But" is the fear, doubt, and hurt that makes it hard to pursue the dream. While identifying and working with the "Buts" like this doesn't make them go away, it does help free us to pursue our dreams, even though we have our fears, doubts, and hurts. Our "Buts" are there, AND they do not have to keep us from our dreams.

You can find a blank copy of the worksheet in the appendix at the end of the book to help you as you set your goals.

Tool #2: Effective Communication

"Don't worry that children never listen to you;
worry that they are always watching you."
Robert Fulghum

Along the way, you will want to be able to communicate effectively with your child. Is there something you would like to talk about with your child right now? Think of a subject to use as an example if you don't have an immediate need. Get a piece of paper or note card and a pen or pencil. Don't use your phone, laptop, or computer to make notes, as they would be barriers to open connection later.

Write down the topic you want to discuss as a simple statement. State your underlying concern rather than a solution you've already decided on. For example, "I want to talk about keeping our house tidy," instead of "I want you to put your things away when you finish using them." Or, "I want to talk about priorities and use of time," instead of "I want you to do your homework before you play video games."

Now, answer the following questions:

1. How do you aspire to be in the conversation?

    a. Would you like to be calm? Patient? Clear? Kind but firm? What qualities fit your values and would help you be more effective?

        i. Select one quality and write it down underneath your topic.

    b. Now think of a time you had this quality, even a little bit. Recall the experience as vividly as possible. Use as many of your senses as you can. Answer questions such as: "Where was I? Inside or outside? What did it look like? What time of day was it? What was the weather like? Was I sitting or standing or walking? How did the chair or beach or bench feel as I sat or stood or walked? What was I wearing? Were there any noticeable smells?" Remember how you felt both physically and emotionally and recapture that experience as strongly as you can.

    i.   As you recall your experience, you are replaying a mini-movie of success. Give your experience a name, like the title of a movie. *Write down the name of your mini-movie of success beneath the quality you want to have throughout the conversation and the topic.* This will help you capture and hold on to that quality as you interact with your child.

2. What do you hope to accomplish?

    a.   Before you start an important conversation with your boss, a colleague, or even a neighbor, you probably think about what you want to accomplish, yet lots of parents never do this before starting a conversation with their child. Is your purpose to give information, share your thoughts and feelings, solve a problem, offer support or encouragement, or strengthen your relationship?

        i.   *Select the outcome that is most important to you and write it down below the other things you've already listed.* Keep this note in front of you throughout the conversation and remind yourself often what you are trying to accomplish and how you aspire to be regardless of how your child chooses to be.

Now, put it all together.

1. Turn off your cell phone. (Yes, we really mean it. Turn it off!) Invite your child to talk with you and let her know she has your full attention.
2. Tell your child what you would like to discuss. If solving a problem or making a decision is part of what you want to accomplish, explain that you are going to take those off the table until you both have had a chance to speak and be heard.
3. Invite your child to go first and tell you her thoughts, feelings, and desires about the topic.
4. Listen with great empathy. See the world through her eyes. What she is feeling and thinking makes sense to her. Look at the world from her perspective, and then speak her reality out loud, especially when it is different from your own.
5. Be curious, ask clarifying questions, recap often and respectfully, and stay focused on her. She needs to feel that you are sincere and caring, not just parroting her words back to her. Let her know that all of her thoughts, feelings, and desires are OK. Make it safe for her to be honest and open with you, even when what she is thinking, feeling, or wanting is uncomfortable or not what you were hoping for.
6. Keep in mind what you want to accomplish and how you aspire to be in this conversation regardless of how she chooses to be.
7. When she is finished, speak with clarity about your own thoughts, feelings, and desires.
8. Take turns, going back and forth as long as needed to get meaningful understanding. *Remember that understanding does not mean agreeing.*
9. If you are looking for solutions or making a decision, now is the time to get some ideas out on the table.

a. Ask your child for her ideas about possible solutions or decisions. Ask her to explain how her ideas honor and respect her concerns and desires as well as yours.

b. Present a few ideas of your own, along with your explanation of how you think they take into account her thoughts, feelings, and desires as well as your own.

c. As the parent, it is always your responsibility to make final decisions, yet consider your child's input as much as you can. Adapt and allow her more influence as she matures.

d. Make your decision and discuss it with her.

10. Whatever the purpose of the conversation, always end with a sincere expression of respect, caring, or appreciation.

Come back and review this sequence often as you practice becoming a more resilient family. At the end of the book there is a worksheet to help you bring your best self to the table when you communicate.

Tool #3: Emotional Grounding

"Speak when you are angry—and you'll make the best speech you'll ever regret."
Laurence J. Peter

Sometimes your child is going to be too upset to have a reasonable conversation—or it might even be you who is too upset! When we feel hurt, scared, or angry, the primitive, self-defensive part of our brains is quick to take over and protect us with a fight, flight, or freeze response. The slower, more newly evolved rational parts of our brain—including our problem-solving and language centers—can get dialed way down. This is probably meant to protect us so that we don't use reason to talk ourselves out of defending ourselves when faced with actual physical danger. It also means that we sometimes end up saying or doing hurtful things we don't really mean when we are upset.

Anne frequently helps her clients understand this by telling them this story about her daughter Ally's experience.

When Ally was in college, she was a wildland firefighter in the summer. An important thing for you to know is that at this time in her life, Ally was a dedicated vegan and seriously committed to protecting all animal life. One day, she and her crew were dropped by helicopter into the backcountry to fight a serious fire. She was using a pickaxe to clear away some brush and establish a fire break. As she swung into the brush, she uncovered a rattlesnake, which reared up in strike pose. When Ally called to tell me about it later, she said that by the time she had the thought, "OMG, there's a rattlesnake!" she had already used her axe to chop off its head.

This is fight, flight, or freeze mode working perfectly. Axe in hand, the primitive brain quickly recognized the danger of the striking snake, turned down the slower, more newly evolved rational part of the brain, and effectively prompted her to use her axe and chop off the snake's head without thinking it through logically. Her brain protected her by switching to fight, flight, or freeze mode, making sure she didn't talk herself into feeling sorry for the snake and protecting it over herself.

When any of us, parents and children alike, feel in danger *physically or emotionally*, we are naturally programmed to respond with fight, flight, or freeze. Wise parents understand this and protect all family members from "chopping" each other's heads off verbally (and physically!).

All families need a clear plan for managing strong emotions. An essential component of this plan is teaching and modeling emotional grounding skills. Emotional grounding is anything you do to bring your emotions down to a manageable level so the rational part of your brain can be fully engaged and you can interact with each other in the best possible way.

For most of us, on a scale of 1 to 10, with 10 being the strongest emotion you can imagine, we are likely to be flooded with a fight, flight, or freeze response when we are at a 6 or higher. Once a fight, flight, or freeze response has been triggered, our brain signals the release of stress chemicals, which tamp down our higher levels of thought and reason. It takes our bloodstream 20 minutes to reabsorb these stress chemicals, allowing more logical thoughts to return.

This is why you need to take a 20-minute break once anyone in the family feels emotionally flooded. At first, while you are learning to calm yourselves, you may need a little more time, but work towards being able to calm down in about 20 minutes. During the break, parents and children alike need to spend the time doing emotional grounding. If we spend the break time working ourselves up, getting more and more upset, we will still be flooded when the 20 minutes are over. By grounding during the break, we maximize the chance that we can have the conversation we need to have instead of more distress. This is so important. Please model grounding, even if you think you don't need it or think you don't have time. It is worth the time and will dramatically change the way your family gets along.

Since it's much less likely that we will hurt anyone or verbally "chop off" any heads while we are grounded, it's essential to have grounding strategies ready to go when stress hits. Below are a few of Anne's favorite emotional grounding techniques she teaches to her clients. You can learn them yourself and then teach them to your child. To use them effectively during your breaks, you and your child will need to practice them over and over again *while you are calm*. This makes them become automatic so you can use them even when you are upset. Anne suggests practicing your favorite grounding techniques while you are calm for three minutes three times a day for at least 27 days. That's how long it takes to make something a solid habit.

- **Come to your senses.** This technique uses our basic senses to bring us into the present moment. Begin with vision. Look around you. Without making any judgments, such as I like or don't like, name five things you can see. For example, "I see two red pillows, a clock, three windows, a chair, and a picture on the wall." Now move on to five things you can hear. "I hear the air conditioner, a car, the clock ticking, birds, and the wind in the trees." Next, touch. "I can feel the pen in my hand, the tag of my shirt, the chair I'm sitting on, my feet in my shoes, and the pillow I'm leaning against." These three senses can be done anywhere, anytime, without anyone even knowing you are doing it. Depending on where you are, you can also use taste and smell. If you get through all of the senses and still feel distressed, go through the list again naming four things, then three, two, and one. If you are still distressed, start over with five and keep going until you feel a sense of calm.
- **Practice 7/11 breathing.** Breathe in, and while you breathe in, count to seven in your head (slowly like you are counting for hide and seek, but silently in your head so you can also breathe). Pause at seven, then slowly breathe out, counting to eleven as you do. While you are breathing and counting, you are relaxing your body and taking a mini-vacation from thinking. No one can think about their troubles and count at the same time!
- **Play some mental games.** Try reading backwards, making lists of your favorite foods, bands, or cars, finding pictures

of places you would like to visit, or counting how many animals you can think of that start with the letter B.

- **Do something active.** (But not aggressive, as being aggressive keeps the stress chemicals going). Go for a walk, take a bike ride, shoot a basketball, or do some yoga stretches.
- **Try something soothing.** Put a warm washcloth on your face, splash your hands in cool water, take a bath, massage your face and neck, read a book, or listen to soothing music.

Create a clear plan to manage strong emotions.

1. Recognize when you or your child is feeling under attack.
2. Take a break to let emotions cool and allow rational thought and good verbal skills to come back online.
3. During your break, use emotional grounding techniques.
4. After your grounding break, always go back and have the conversation you were going to have, bringing your best self to the table, as outlined above in Tool #2: Effective Communication. This demonstrates your integrity and commitment and will strengthen your relationship and build family resiliency.

You can find worksheets of these tools at the back of the book.

Chapter 3

GRATITUDE

"Gratitude is not only the greatest of virtues, but the parent of all the others."
Marcus Tullius Cicero

PANCAKES FOR MOM AND DAD: EVERYDAY GRATITUDE

"When you arise in the morning, give thanks for the morning light, for your life and strength. Give thanks for your food, and the joy of living. If you see no reason for giving thanks, the fault lies with yourself."
Tecumseh, Shawnee chief

Gratitude is a sense of thankfulness and joy that comes from noticing that something positive has come into your life from a source outside of yourself, whether you attribute that source to another person, God, nature, the universe, or something else. Cultures around the world and throughout time have recognized that cultivating a sense of gratitude is related to many positive benefits, both short- and long-term. Being grateful now helps us feel better in the moment and builds a kind of reserve that can help us get through difficult times in the future as well. In other words, it helps us develop greater resiliency.

In recent years, researchers have put gratitude to the test to see if it really is all it has been cracked up to be. Here are some of the positive emotional, psychological, social, and physical benefits they have found:

- Heightened sense of well-being
- Reduced negative affect and increased positive affect
- More positive and optimistic appraisals of life
- More time spent exercising
- Fewer negative physical symptoms
- More sleep and better quality sleep
- An increase in how often people help someone else with a personal problem or offer emotional support to another
- A greater sense of connectedness to others

Think about this little boy's classic experience...

A six-year-old boy wanted to do something special for his parents, so he decided he would surprise them with a pancake breakfast. Early Saturday morning, he quietly got up to start his special surprise. His journey began with pushing a chair up to the cupboard to get the mixing bowl, flour, and sugar. Next, he went to the refrigerator for milk and eggs, and put everything on the kitchen table to mix the ingredients. Before long, he had dropped the flour on the floor, knocked the egg carton off the table, spilled a cup of milk, poured too much sugar in the bowl, chased the cat out of the kitchen, and slipped in the mess on the floor. He crashed into the table, hit the edge of the bowl, and spilled the contents all over himself and the floor. The noise awakened his father, who got out of bed and went to the kitchen to investigate. The little boy saw his father, started crying, and ran to his dad, who picked him up and gave him a big hug. The boy explained what he was trying to do, and the father hugged him again, this time tighter in loving recognition of his generous heart. The boy's father didn't mind getting the mess all over him in the process. Rather than getting angry, he helped his son clean up the mess and make pancakes for his mother.

At the moment the father entered the kitchen, all that his son wanted and needed was a reassuring hug and simple appreciation of his good intent and efforts to do his very best. The value of such a hug is amazing, and the impact it has on each of us is staggering. Current research tells us that hugs are one of the necessities of life. It has been said, "A hug is a universal medicine; it is how we handshake from the heart." It's hard to beat a good, solid hug for saying, "I love you. You are special." The great family therapist Virginia Satir said that we need four hugs a day for survival, we need eight hugs a day for maintenance, and we need 12 hugs a day for growth.

Parenting Strategy

When was the last time you gave your child a hug? How many hugs do you usually give your child each day? If you are already giving plenty of heartfelt hugs, please keep it up! Your child will never outgrow the need, no matter how old she is. If hugs haven't been a regular part of your family, it is never too late to start. Start softly, maybe just a gentle squeeze on the shoulder. Gradually build up to stronger, more full-bodied hugs, given more and more frequently. Notice, appreciate, and savor your gratitude for the joy of being connected with your child. Enjoy! You are building resilience for today and stockpiling a reserve of "bounce forward" strength for the future.

GIRL FROM MOROCCO: REJOICE FOR WHAT YOU HAVE

"He is a wise man who does not grieve for the things which he has not, but rejoices for those which he has."
Epictetus

It can be tempting to compare ourselves and our situations with others and to think the world unfair or feel jealous. As tempting as it is, however, there is little reason to believe such an approach will lead you and your family to a greater sense of well-being. Focusing on gratitude for all that you do have is much more likely to lead you to a fulfilling and resilient life. You will better enjoy each present moment and build a reserve of resiliency to help you face whatever the future has in store.

Cal's Story

It was December of 2011 and my son and I were in Morocco with my grandson, who was completing his Boy Scout Eagle Project. My son and his family were living in Stuttgart, Germany at that time, and my grandson learned that the children in an orphanage in Meknes, Morocco needed clothing. He held a fundraiser and earned enough money to purchase one item of clothing for each child. He invited his dad and me to accompany him when he went to the orphanage.

While we were in Morocco, we spent a few days touring the countryside. One day, as we stopped at a red light, a cute little girl who appeared to be about nine years old approached the car and wanted to sell us flowers. My son rolled down his window to explain that we couldn't use the flowers. This little girl pled with her eyes, which made it difficult to say no, but we were determined. When the light changed, we started to drive off, but this little girl was well trained and knew exactly what to do next. She threw her bouquet of flowers into the car. What could we do but stop, laugh, and give this persistent little girl some money for the flowers?

I have often thought about this little girl and wondered where she is, what she is doing, how life is going for her, if she is happy. I will never know the answers, but this experience made me more appreciative of my family and my life. We are so fortunate that our children and grandchildren have good schools to attend, safe homes, opportunities to play sports or musical instruments, well-trained doctors and quality health care, and protection from many of the problems that the little Moroccan girl likely encountered daily.

Yet my family is not necessarily any happier than this young girl who seemed to be grateful for the little bit of money she got for her flowers. Gratitude for what we have is a powerful way of living, regardless of our circumstances.

Parenting Strategy

When your child brings up something he doesn't have that he wants, spend a couple of minutes talking about how nice it would be to have that new bike, new friend, chance to go skiing, or date to the prom. Acknowledge his hopes and desires. There is nothing wrong with wanting more or dreaming big. The problems come when we focus too much on what we *don't have* and not enough on gratitude for what we *do have*. Help your child *balance* his focus by spending at least as much energy on being truly mindful of and grateful for what he does have as he spends wishing for what he doesn't have.

Get two big posters or poster-size Post-it notes that you can put up on the wall or a door, and start to make two lists: a gratitude list and a list of desires. Another way to do this is with two boxes and slips of paper to write on and drop in the boxes. Whatever way you do it, the idea is to make sure that your gratitude list is at least as long as your desire list. Start by asking your child to think of things for which he is grateful. Follow up by asking him to think of all of the things he desires. Add some of the things for which you are grateful and some of the things you want. Talk about how each of you feels as you work on the lists. Keep adding to your lists for a few days. Keep noticing how you feel as you focus on each list. How is your balance?

A QUICK ERRAND: EXPRESS GRATITUDE

"Forget injuries, never forget kindness."
Confucius

Think about your child's life. How often does she express gratitude right now? Research shows that when people increase their expression of gratitude, they start to benefit immediately. Which of the benefits of gratitude do you think would help your child the most? Would you like her to feel a greater sense of well-being? Have less negativity in her life, or more frequent and stronger positive emotions? Feel more optimistic about her life? Get more exercise, and have fewer aches and pains or physical complaints? Get more sleep, and feel more refreshed? Be more involved with others and feel more connected? How much would these benefits improve your child's life right now?

And what about her future? Surely, she will face challenges. That is a given in life. Increasing her expression of gratitude will help her build a deep reserve of strength on which she can draw when problems come. Set the example and help your child make it a habit to regularly express gratitude.

Cal's Story

When I walked in the front door, I could smell the hamburger my first wife, Carol, was cooking for the spaghetti she was preparing. I was hungry and ready to eat, but it wasn't quite done, so we decided to run a quick errand. We gathered up our son, loaded him into the car, and left. Unfortunately, when we arrived at our destination, the merchandise we ordered was not ready, so the quick errand turned into more than an hour. By this time, we were hungry and anxious to get home.

As we entered our subdivision, we noticed a lot of excitement, with people running towards some unknown destination. We were curious but didn't think much about it until we noticed they were running down our street. When we turned onto our street, we saw a fire truck in front of our house. Neighbors, friends, and strangers were all congregating, watching the firefighters. There was no place to park, so I left the car in the middle of the street, jumped out, and took off running to my house. I wished I had not been in such a hurry, because I arrived just in time to watch a firefighter walk through the door carrying a frying pan of smoking hamburger.

I was grateful for the action of my backdoor neighbor, a firefighter, who took it upon himself to save our home when he saw the smoke billowing out of our kitchen window. I thanked him and told him how much his actions meant to my family and me. He said that he was just glad he was there and knew what to do. I have often thought how fortunate we were, and how easily we could have prevented that situation by simply taking a moment to turn off the stove before we left.

Parenting Strategy

Are you personally willing to experiment with gratitude? In formal research studies, participants receive specific instructions to follow, such as keeping a daily gratitude journal, writing thank you letters, giving a certain number of verbal appreciations daily, or listening to structured gratitude meditations. Wherever you are right now, what do you have to lose by increasing your practice of gratitude? If you accept the challenge, you will see for yourself how it impacts your own sense of well-being. At the same time, you'll gain experience and become a strong role model for your child.

If you decide to experiment, ask yourself what measurable action you will take. Think about the different ways of focusing on gratitude listed above and which one interests you the most. Would you like to keep a gratitude journal, write thank you letters, verbally tell people how grateful you are for them, or listen to guided meditations? Choose one, and then select when you will practice gratitude. Will you focus on gratitude first thing in the morning, or think back at the end of the day? It's easier to start a new habit if you tie it to routines you already have, such as right after breakfast, after school, or just before bed. Committing to a specific action at a specific time of day greatly increases the likelihood that you will follow through and experience the benefits for yourself and be ready to share this powerful resiliency skill with your child.

Share your journey with your child. Invite her to join you. Tell her about the things for which you are truly grateful today. Think of new things each day instead of just saying the same thing over and over again. Ask her what she is grateful for today. Talk about it together. Tell each other the story behind your gratitude. Did something happen to make you notice it today? What does it mean to you or how does it bless your life? "I was so tired and grumpy this morning and then, happy day, we had enough bread to make everyone's lunch! Today, I am grateful for having bread."

Keep a record and post it where it can be seen. It can be a simple list, pictures your child draws or cuts out of a magazine, or whatever suits her age and interests. Don't put it off until you get something snazzy. It is more important to just get started. You can always go back and decorate it or make it more durable later. Remember, sharing gratitude and making it public strengthens it.

BUCKET OF ROCKS: IT'S NEVER TOO LATE

"The single greatest thing you can do to change your life today would be to start being grateful for what you have right now. And the more grateful you are, the more you get."
Oprah Winfrey

Noticing the good in life and expressing gratitude for it intensifies the positive emotions we are already having. The overall experience therefore becomes increasingly pleasurable. Grateful people then feel better longer and more intensely, not necessarily because more good things are happening to them, but because gratitude heightens and prolongs each positive experience. In addition, at any time in the future, they can bring to mind their gratitude, which again amplifies the experience, potentially by an infinite amount, as they can feel the pleasant sensation of gratitude warming their heart anytime they choose to recall it.

Sometimes, however, we fail to notice, or perhaps to realize, that a certain experience, which might not feel so wonderful at the time, might in fact turn out to be something for which, in hindsight, we become truly grateful. It is never too late to cultivate gratitude for any experience and begin to reap the benefits.

Cal's Story

As a young boy, I loved to spend time with my cousins, playing on Grandpa's farm and generally getting into the usual boyhood trouble. One summer, I managed to get into more trouble than usual. Let's just say it might have involved falling off a horse, dislocating my elbow, having surgery, getting my cast wet while I may or may not have been playing with my cousins in an irrigation ditch, and having to sit in the hot sun all afternoon to dry out my cast.

Dr. Worthen was the country doctor who treated my arm, and, after finally taking off my cast, he suggested to Grandma that I should carry a milk bucket full of rocks all around the farm. He explained this would help straighten my arm. The torture began as soon as I got home. Under Grandma's watchful eyes and vocal supervision (e.g., "Calvert! Pick up that bucket!"), or under the eyes of my aunts who lived just down the road and were Grandma's allies, I hauled rocks everywhere I went. By the end of summer, I thought the bucket was an extension of my right arm. While I hated doing it, I have to admit it worked.

As a result of Dr. Worthen's rock therapy, my arm healed with minimal permanent damage. When the cast initially came off, I could only straighten my arm approximately 25%. After a summer of rock hauling, I could straighten it about 95%. Today's doctors would probably recognize what a great job Dr. Worthen and Grandma Cazier did to rehabilitate my arm and wholeheartedly support and applaud their actions. Personally, I am grateful now to both of them, and especially to Grandma, who had the hardest job.

Grandma taught me the reward of diligence, as well as obedience. I didn't want to carry those rocks, but I am glad I did. I wonder if I told her how grateful I was that she made me carry the milk bucket with rocks. I doubt I expressed my appreciation to her. I didn't really realize my good fortune or appreciate what she had done for me at the time, and later, I'm sorry to say, I think I just assumed she knew.

Parenting Strategy

Tell your child a story about something you did not fully appreciate at the time, but for which you became truly grateful only later. Ask yourself if there is a way to show gratitude now. If possible, sit down with your child and write a letter of gratitude or send a picture, a card, or some other small token of appreciation you and your child choose.

Maybe you can't actually say thank you to the person because, like Cal's grandma, the person has already passed away, or maybe a stranger helped you and you don't know the person's name or how to contact them. Whether or not you can say thank you to that person, write the story down together, draw pictures, or record it however makes sense depending on your child's age and interests. Create a way for you and your child to share the story with three other people. You could read it out loud to the person or to his or her descendants, share it with friends or family, submit it to a local newspaper, or post it on Facebook.

Research shows that thinking about gratitude increases a person's overall sense of well-being and satisfaction. Writing it down is even more powerful, and speaking it out loud and sharing it with another person is the most powerful of all. Teaching your child to be grateful and express his gratitude will help him become more resilient, be better prepared to face his own hard times, be of service to others, and enjoy the benefits of gratitude.

THE SNOWSHOE HIKE: LET US BE THANKFUL

"Let us rise up and be thankful, for if we didn't learn a lot today, at least we learned a little, and if we didn't learn a little, at least we didn't get sick, and if we got sick, at least we didn't die; so, let us all be thankful."
Buddha

Every day, all day long, we create stories in our heads about our experiences. Generally, we each have habits about the way we interpret our experiences and the kinds of stories we tell ourselves about life. For example, George, as a 16-year-old boy, may have the habit of noticing any slights, and the story he tells himself in his head about the party he went to last night emphasizes that nobody noticed him when he first came in the door, his friends didn't come over to say hi, and the girl he likes spent more time talking to some other guy than to him.

Lay a foundation for gratitude by making it a habit to notice both the good and not-so-good things that happen. This is not to suggest simply looking on the bright side and ignoring the negative. This is about paying accurate attention to the totality of experience and incorporating that into the stories we make in our heads. A more balanced awareness makes cultivating gratitude easier.

Cal's Story

When I was 16 or 17 years old, I went with my Boy Scout troop on an overnight snowshoe hike to a cabin in the mountains. We were all excited and full of enthusiasm. We piled our equipment onto the trucks, and off we went. After a short drive, we finally started our hike up the mountain. The cabin belonged to an uncle of one of the boys. Some of us had been there in the winter several years before, but we quickly became disoriented in the snowy terrain. We wandered around the mountain, trying to find the cabin. I was hiking beside a friend, who slipped and fell, then he fell again, then he fell again, over and over, more and more frequently until he was falling every few steps.

On closer examination, we realized he was wearing engineer boots, similar to cowboy boots, which were definitely not warm, waterproof, or appropriate for the activity. The leaders had prepared a list of equipment that each of us was required to bring and had gone through a pre-hike inspection. Proper boots were at the top, but somehow he had managed to escape the scout master's eagle eye. We pulled off his boots and discovered that they were packed with ice and his feet were frozen. Our leaders recognized the danger and knew something needed to be done quickly or he might lose one or both feet. About 50 yards from where we were, we saw a cabin and decided to break into it to save his feet. As he began to thaw, we warmed up some food and ate. One of the leaders, a couple of my friends, and I went back down the mountain for help.

Everything worked out well. Help arrived in time, and my friend's feet were saved. We notified the owner of the cabin about the break-in, and he was very gracious and even offered to let us use his cabin again, provided we didn't break in next time! The next summer, we returned and fixed the damage we caused. We were very grateful that help had been available when we needed it and that all would be well.

We will all make mistakes and need others to rescue us and forgive us. We can help our children develop greater resiliency by teaching them to be grateful for the help they receive and the personal growth they can gain by learning valuable lessons through their life experiences.

Parenting Strategy

We choose the story we tell ourselves about each of our experiences. Cal could have chosen to focus on how cold and miserable it was that day, or on how dumb the leaders were to get lost or let a boy start out so poorly equipped. Instead, he chose to focus on the equally true story of gratitude: gratitude that the leaders noticed a boy in trouble, gratitude that they found a safe place to get out of the cold, gratitude that they were able to get the help they needed, gratitude that no one came to any real harm.

What stories are you teaching your child to tell about her life? As you think about what happened today, help your child tell the truth about the hard things in life and find the things for which she can be truly grateful:

- "I fell off my bike and got banged up pretty bad, and I'm so grateful I didn't get hurt any worse."
- "I missed six words on my spelling test, and I'm so grateful I get another chance this week to study harder or prepare myself better."
- "I'm so sad I didn't get that job, and I learned some things I can use in my next interview."

Nurturing a sense of gratitude is an essential part of building resiliency.

Chapter 4

FORGIVENESS

"Life is an adventure in forgiveness."
Norman Cousins

Ambrose Stole Some Apples: The Power of Forgiveness

"Forgiveness is a catalyst creating the atmosphere necessary
for a fresh start and a new beginning."
Martin Luther King, Jr.

Let's face it: no one is perfect and we all need forgiveness. None of us want to be defined by the worst thing we've ever done, and we've all done things we wish we had not. As a parent, you have the opportunity to help your child learn about the power of forgiveness.

Very simply stated, forgiveness is a choice. It is a free gift given to someone who has harmed you, whether or not they deserve it, because you choose to let go of your rights to resentment and revenge. To better understand what forgiveness is, it helps to understand what forgiveness is *not*.

Forgiveness is *not*:

- Condoning harmful behavior
- Ignoring an offense
- Removing consequences
- Automatic regaining of trust
- Instant emotional healing
- Instant restoration of the same relationship
- Forgetting (which is not really possible, but forgiveness does mean choosing not to keep bringing up the offense, especially in anger, not to hold it over the other, and not to use it as leverage)

As you help your child learn about forgiveness, why he needs it, how to ask for it, and how to give it, he will learn that even though he cannot change the past, he can shape the present and the future. In the process of giving and receiving forgiveness, he can become part of the solution. He can realize that, with forgiveness, mistakes are not the end of the story but the beginning of a new chapter, one that he can write. As he writes his new chapters, he will become more resilient, better able to take the missteps and pains of life in stride, and better equipped to move forward stronger, more confident, and more capable.

Cal's Story

My grandfather Ambrose Call grew up in Bountiful, Utah, during the early 1890s. He was 82 years old when I sat on his floor, enthralled for two-plus hours, listening to his life history. He told me about the time he and his friends stole some apples from an elderly man's orchard. At first, nothing happened, and the boys felt pretty confident that they had gotten away without being caught. A few days later, however, as Ambrose sat with his family in church, this same old man slowly and painfully rose from his seat, haltingly made his way to the podium, and addressed the congregation. "As you all know, I make a small living from my little apple orchard, and now I'm in trouble because some of my apples are missing. I caught just a glimpse of some boys running from the orchard the other day, and I wonder if maybe they are the ones who stole my apples." Ambrose squirmed in his seat but said nothing.

That afternoon, while eating their meal, Ambrose's father asked him, "Were you involved with the boys who stole that man's apples?" Ashamed, but also relieved, Ambrose admitted that he was. This admission led to a father-and-son discussion about what Ambrose could do to correct the problem. They agreed that he would ask forgiveness and repay the man, and they put the plan into action right then and there.

The solitary walk to the old man's home somehow seemed longer than that same path had seemed just a few days earlier with his friends, laughing and joking around when they had the impulsive idea to steal some apples. Now, one deliberate, dread-filled step followed another until, at last, Ambrose stood on the old man's porch, his hand trembling as he reached out to knock on the door and seal his fate. Imagine his surprise when the old man graciously invited him in and asked him to sit down. The words tumbled out of Ambrose's mouth: "I am so sorry. I didn't think. Please forgive me. Is there any way I can pay you back?"

As if in a dream, Ambrose's feet sped home, light and quick, free from guilt and shame. As agreed, early Saturday morning, Ambrose returned once again. This time, he stayed all day, picking apples and safely storing them in the old man's cellar where they belonged. At the end of the day, he had picked 20 bushels of apples, and, more importantly, he had developed a friendship with a good man, which lasted until the old man's death.

Parenting Strategy

Some things change; others don't. Most children today do not live in small farming communities or walk past apple orchards with their friends, but they can still experience the same warm feeling of forgiveness and learn the value of honesty and a clear conscience that comes from making things right again after harming someone else.

The key? Practice. Practice. Practice. Practicing giving and receiving forgiveness in small, daily events will help your child develop his "forgiveness muscle," so that when someone hurts him in a major way or he hurts someone else, he will be prepared. It's like the difference between preparing for a marathon by running every day for months, or just showing up for the big event and hoping for the best.

Talk about forgiveness every day. As a parent, model forgiving and making sincere, effective apologies. Speak about the little injuries of your life and your choice to let them go. When that guy just cut you off on the freeway, respond by saying, "I choose to forgive him and not let him ruin the rest of the trip." If you forget you promised to help at the school bookfair, say, "I am so sorry I forgot to come. You were counting on me, and I let you down. You have every right to be upset. I hope you will forgive me and give me another chance. Is there something else I can do to help?"

You don't have to wait for something bad to happen. Be proactive about practicing and create opportunities for practice. In the Choose Your Own Adventure series of books by R. A. Montgomery, as each story unfolds, the reader comes to a decision point. Do you want the character in the book to answer the front door or slip out the back? Run down the stairs or hide in the bedroom? Depending on your choice, the books direct you to turn to a certain page and the story continues in different ways. You can read the books over and over again, creating new stories based on the choices you make.

Play "Choose Your Own Adventure" with your child, using the hurts and mistakes you see going on around him as your opening text. When you see a little boy grab his baby brother's toy at the grocery store, ask your child to play out various endings with you. What might happen in the next few moments, or even for the rest of the day, if the boy sincerely apologizes and gives back the toy, or if he keeps it and taunts his baby brother, etc.?

Be a great role model of both forgiving and asking for forgiveness. Graciously forgive your child when he does something hurtful, and ask for your child's forgiveness when you make a mistake, miss a cue, or are insensitive. Model it, and then model it again, and again. Remember, forgiveness is *not* condoning bad behavior or removing consequences. Scale your response to the severity of the offense. Use each incident as a chance for you and your child to learn and grow stronger and more resilient. With this preparation, your child will be ready to make well-considered choices when he is hurt or makes mistakes of his own. He will feel comfortable talking with you about any aspect of forgiveness. He will understand the value of seeking and giving forgiveness and will know how to create new beginnings. At times, you will fall short, and your child will fall short. That's to be expected. Just get up, and try again. That is what resiliency is all about.

Happy failing forward!

BETRAYAL: LEARNING FROM PAIN

"An eye for an eye only makes the whole world blind."
Mahatma Gandhi

Forgiveness is both a choice and a skill that can be developed. Like all skills, the more you practice, the more skillful you become. Like all skills, your child might wonder, "Will it be worth it to me? This is a lot of work, so what's the benefit?" As your child becomes more skillful with forgiveness, she will also develop increased self-esteem, happiness, hope, a sense of freedom, lightness, joy, and overall well-being. If she does not learn forgiveness, she will likely become more angry, hostile, anxious, and depressed.

Your child may resist forgiving others because when she feels hurt, she wants them to take the first step. She wants them to admit they are wrong, apologize, and make amends. This would, of course, be ideal, but in reality it often just doesn't happen. This is where choice comes in. The person who hurt your child may never feel bad about what he or she did, may never apologize (or might not mean it if he or she does), or may never try to repair the damage. When your child chooses to wait until the other person "deserves" to be forgiven, she continues to carry the burden of hurt and resentment, and every minute she carries that burden, she is letting the other person hurt her again, and again, and again.

The other option is choosing forgiveness, whether or not the other person deserves it. With this choice, your child claims the power to make things right inside her own heart and mind. She chooses not to let the other person keep hurting her. She chooses to let go of bitterness and pain. She chooses to learn what she can from the experience and move on stronger and more confident.

An important part of moving on is deciding whether or not to reconnect with or trust the other person again. Many people think that forgiving someone always means letting the other person back into your life. Actually, forgiving and reconnecting are two separate things. In order to be free of the burden of bitterness and pain, your child will not only need to forgive everyone who hurts her but will also need the wisdom to discern who she can safely let back into her life and who would harm her again and should not be let back in. Your child is fortunate to have you in her corner as she learns and practices these essential skills of a resilient life.

Anne's Story

My first husband had a great career opportunity in the Bay Area, so we said our goodbyes to friends and family and made the move. Being new in the community, of course we were eager to make new friends. We started inviting people to get together with our family including our youngest daughter, who moved to California with us. We invited people to go for a bike ride, a hike, or a meal. One day, we invited an intelligent, interesting woman who was about our age over for dinner. She was single with a young son, who also joined. One invitation led to another, and a family friendship began to grow.

The whole story gets quite complicated from here, far beyond the scope of this short tale. What you do need to know is that both our marriage and the family friendship we had started developing began to take a backseat to a growing connection between my husband and our friend. After seeking help from a wonderful counselor, many long and tearful talks, and promises made and broken again and again, my husband and I ended our 29-year marriage. He and our friend married three days after our divorce became final. They didn't even tell me or our daughters of their wedding until after the fact.

The next few years were hard ones for me in many ways. It was a time of grief and loss. Our youngest daughter was starting college and moved into her own apartment. I lived alone for the first time in my adult life. This was not the life plan I had expected. My marriage vows meant a great deal to me. I believed marriage meant staying together through good times and bad and finding ways to move forward that work for both people, yet this was not possible.

I discovered I was stronger than I had known. I leaned on friends and family, but I was also able to be there for them when they had their own troubles. I strengthened my relationships, made new ones, learned to cook for one, and managed my finances and household on my own. I advanced in my career and created a life for myself.

I learned more about forgiveness than I ever thought I would need to know. I went to therapy and worked on forgiving myself for my shortcomings. Step-by-step, I made progress forgiving my ex-husband and his new wife. I came to know in a very deep way that forgiving someone who has hurt or betrayed you is the most important thing you can do. It doesn't mean you are weak or that the harm isn't real and lasting. It does mean that you can accept what has already happened, choose to forgive, remember over and over again that you chose to forgive, and finally begin to feel the burden of hurt and anger lifting from your life.

My ex-husband and his second wife were married only a short time, and then they divorced. Several years later, the woman contacted me. I had long since moved to Salt Lake City, Utah, started my own private therapy practice, and met and married my wonderful Cal. She said that she was coming to town and asked if I would agree to meet with her. We met for breakfast at a small cafe not far from our home. She said she had come to understand what happened in a new light, offered what seemed to be a sincere apology, and asked me to forgive her. I told her that I had forgiven both my ex-husband and her a long time ago. She expressed surprise and said that she did not know that. I explained that forgiving her was not for her sake, but for my own. I forgave her because I did not want the burden of feeling angry or bitter about events that were over and done.

After expressing relief and gratitude for being forgiven, she started to talk about my ex-husband in a negative and blaming sort of way. I asked her to stop and told her that although my ex undoubtedly had his faults, I had no desire to discuss them with her. For me, forgiving someone means that when thoughts of old hurts come to mind, I remind myself that I have chosen to forgive and work to let the thoughts go rather than dwell on them. When I find this to be difficult, I turn to Cal and other trusted friends to help me work through it. Although I truly forgave her in the sense that I held no ill will towards her, I did not trust her and did not want to chat with her about anything—let alone about my ex-husband—nor did I want to become friends again. We parted, and I have not heard from her or seen her since.

I am not happy that my first marriage ended the way that it did, but out of that pain and sorrow, I have gained much personal growth and so many beautiful opportunities for love and happiness that I would not trade for anything.

Parenting Strategy

Anne could have created a great grievance story out of these experiences. Instead, she chose to live in keeping with her values: friendships, loving family, hard work, progress, education, and career. The insight and wisdom she gained continue to shape her life. She learned much about fairness, trust, commitment, and respect for others. She keeps these lessons in mind as she listens with deeper empathy to the hurts and trials of her clients and walks the long path to forgiveness with them. This does not mean that what happened was somehow OK because good came out of it. It does mean that, like Anne, your child can develop the resiliency to choose forgiveness and bounce forward.

Break down forgiveness into manageable, understandable steps, and teach those steps to your child. Each of these steps will help your child to build courage and resolve, and she will be better able to face whatever challenges come her way with greater and greater resiliency.

When something hurtful happens, guide your child in how to move forward by going through each step of forgiveness. Here is a breakdown of the steps of forgiveness you can teach your child:

1. Allow yourself some time to feel your hurt, pain, loss, or grief. Acknowledge the depth of your experience.
2. Seek out a couple of trusted people and share your story. Ask them to comfort you and be a witness to your pain. Don't gossip or tell everyone.
3. Think about why it is hard to forgive, and ask yourself if you are ready to choose forgiveness. If you are not ready yet, ask yourself what you need to do to become ready. (This is not about the other person making any changes; this is about your personal growth.)
4. When you are ready, choose forgiveness.
5. Make a clear commitment to let go of your rights to resentment and revenge.
6. For any significant hurt, make a tangible record of your choice to forgive. Here are some ideas:

a. Write down your choice and put it where it will remind you of your decision.

b. Place a note or symbol of your choice to forgive inside a box, and then gift wrap the box.

c. Write a forgiveness letter to the other person, which you may or may not send.

    i. Describe how you were affected by what the other person did to you.

    ii. Tell the other person what you wish he or she had done instead.

    iii. Make a clear statement that you choose to forgive the other person with no strings attached.

7. When thoughts of the hurt come up, remind yourself of your choice to forgive.

8. Choose to refocus on qualities and behaviors you value that enrich your life. Many people find it helpful to focus on love, gratitude, service, beauty, and acts of kindness.

9. Think deeply about the wisdom of choosing to reconnect, or not, with the person who hurt you. Seek advice from a couple of people you trust as you think through this important choice. Maybe you will choose to discuss your decision with the same people with whom you shared your story earlier or maybe with someone else. Forgiveness does not mean putting yourself in a position in which you will be hurt over and over again.

10. Repeat, repeat, repeat these steps as often as needed.

THE BLUE PLATE SPECIAL: EMPATHY IN ACTION

"A good apology is like antibiotic, a bad apology is like rubbing salt in the wound."
Randy Pausch

Empathy is an essential part of forgiveness. What is empathy? Being able to really see the world through someone else's eyes and to know how another person thinks, feels, and responds. Your child is more likely to forgive when he truly understands another person's perspective.

Before your child can understand and appreciate another person's feelings, he needs to understand and respect his own feelings. You can help him by accepting and honoring all of his feelings. Yes, all of them. Make it safe for him to feel and tell you about the "bad" feelings, like hurt, fear, sadness, and anger, as well as the "good" feelings, like happiness, excitement, calmness, and joy. Help him learn to recognize what he is feeling, name his feelings, and express them to you openly and directly. This should always be safe.

Teach him that it is not acceptable to act out on his emotions in ways that harm himself or anyone else. For example, it is reasonable to feel hurt and angry when his friend takes something that belongs to him. It is safe for him to tell you what happened and how he feels. It is appropriate for him to tell his friend that he is hurt and angry and that he wants his friend to give it back to him. It is not acceptable for him to yell, hit, or take something belonging to his friend. There is a difference between feeling emotions, expressing emotions, and acting on emotions.

As your child comes to better understand and express his own emotions, he can also better understand the emotions of others. Help him think through the same process for others that you used to help him think through his own experiences. What happened? What do you think the other person is thinking? What is the other person likely feeling? Can you give the feeling a name? What do you think the other person would like to have happen next? What would help the other person feel better?

With growing empathy, it will be easier for your child to choose to forgive. Being able to forgive will help your child develop the resiliency he needs to face and overcome his stumbling blocks. Imagine the freedom your child will experience when he knows without a doubt that no matter what happens, he can let it go, forgive, and move forward.

Anne's Story

It was a hectic day in the Evans' home, which was not unusual in a big family. The exact details of how it all started have been lost in the shuffle, but one child, whose identity is mercifully forgotten, broke something belonging to another child. Tempers flared and angry words were exchanged. Our mother, Joy, brought all of us kids together and gave us a nice little lecture on the virtue of forgiveness, patiently explaining that accidents and mistakes happen, that we shouldn't let ourselves get upset, that family relationships are more important than material things, etc., etc., etc. You've heard it all before.

It's what happened next that made that day different from all of the rest. Everyone had soon forgotten the squabble, as kids so often do, and were playing happily together when, in the commotion, Mom's beautiful blue plate that was hanging on the wall crashed to the floor. This plate was a gift of love and appreciation from our dad. With tears streaming down her face and pain in her voice, Mom gathered us together once again, and shared her difficult lesson. "It is so much easier," she confessed, "to speak of forgiveness when it is someone else's prized possession." The pain of the loss is real, and that is what makes choosing to forgive so powerful.

Dad glued the plate together as best as he could, and hung it back on the wall. The Blue Plate became a family symbol of putting things in perspective, forgiveness, and love. When Mom passed away in 2012, the patched Blue Plate was one of her cherished possessions, carefully preserved for future generations.

Parenting Strategy

That day, Joy experienced a deep surge of empathy as she really put herself in the other person's shoes. Empathy also puts the ability to forgive on the fast track, even though it may still take some time to get through the feelings of hurt or loss.

Practice seeing the world through others' eyes with your child. Go to the food court at the mall, the park, or any place near you where people gather and walk (licking an ice-cream cone or munching on a crisp apple while you're there can make this even more fun). Take turns with your child picking out people, describing how you think they are feeling, and how you can tell. "I think that little boy is tired and bored. I can tell by how he is whining and dragging his feet." Developing empathy when your child is not upset or involved will make it easier for him to have empathy and choose forgiveness when he is.

When other people aren't there for you to observe, try it the other way around. Ask your child to think about how a small child who is tired and bored might act at the mall or the grocery store. Have him act it out. Now let him think of a scene for you to act out. Be playful and have some fun with this. An older child can tackle more complicated or sophisticated scenarios. How would a 12-year-old girl feel if she was cut from the team? What if a 16-year-old asked someone out and was rejected? What are different ways these kids might act in response to their feelings?

Empathy and forgiveness go hand in hand. Together, they help your child develop a deepening respect for self and others, free him from carrying the burden of grudges and regrets, and strengthen his ability to embrace the opportunities and challenges of life resiliently.

THE GLASS PIANO: APOLOGY ACCEPTED

"A man must be big enough to admit his mistakes, smart enough to profit from them, and strong enough to correct them."
John C. Maxwell

Apologies are an essential part of the forgiveness process. Help your child learn to graciously accept an apology when one is offered after she has been harmed. Like many other people, your child may find it easier to accept the apologies of others and forgive them than to accept her own remorse and fully forgive herself. When your child does not forgive herself, she carries a burden of guilt and shame that can be just as devastating as the burden of resentment and bitterness she carries when she does not forgive others. Forgiving both self and others is vital to moving forward and living life resiliently.

You can help your child free herself from the burdens of guilt and shame by teaching her how to take responsibility in both words and deeds for any pain she causes. Just saying "I'm sorry" is not enough, even in the smallest of offenses. The next step of making appropriate amends is required to complete the repair. Your child will be better able to truly forgive herself when she takes full responsibility, including making amends.

Of course, not all injuries involve damage to a tangible object that can be restored or replaced. Many hurts cannot be healed by repairing something physical, and yet, whatever the harm may be, an important aspect of taking responsibility is making amends to the fullest level possible.

Cal's Story

1974 was a long, hard year. My first wife, Carol, and I were far away from our home, family, and roots in the high mountain valleys of the western United States. I was struggling to finish my education at the University of Tennessee, while doing my best to support Carol through painful surgery and a series of radiation treatments that left her confined to a wheelchair, physically as weak as a kitten. Although she still faced many weeks of treatments yet to come, she was courageous, strong in mind and spirit, resilient, and undaunted in her determination to overcome the ovarian cancer that wracked her young body.

My heart also went out to our little boy, Paul, who was trying to help his mom the best a three-year-old could and to understand what was going on. It was surely a long, hard year for that little guy, too, but we decided in spite of it all to join some friends on an outing to Gatlinburg, Tennessee, a small resort city 40 miles southeast of Knoxville. I pushed Carol along, and, being poor students, we mostly window shopped at the various stores designed to draw in tourists and entice them to part with their money.

Everything came to a standstill when we saw the glass blower. We were mesmerized, watching him transform little blobs of glass into delicate beauty. None of us had ever seen such a thing. Carol fell in love with a miniature glass-blown grand piano. What could we do? We bought it, and it became a treasure that Carol loved and protected.

Years later, long after I graduated and Carol's health slowly improved, Paul was playing in the living room, just tossing around a ball, like he had a thousand times before. This time, the ball missed its target and went straight for the little glass piano, smashing it to pieces. Of course, Carol forgave him, but, oh, the tears she shed for the loss of that little treasure that had come to mean so much to her. Paul felt so sorry and had a guilty conscience about his careless throw.

Over 20 years later, Paul came home to visit us with his wife and his own little kids, bringing a special gift for his mother. Carefully, she opened the unexpected gift, finding another little glass-blown piano inside. Paul knew that his mother had forgiven him, but for all those years, he carried some guilt for the incident. He wanted to let his mother know how much he cared for her. As Carol opened the present, both she and I started to weep, not really for the piano, but for the sensitivity and love of a son for his mother. Carol lovingly placed the little piano safely in her curio. Today, years after cancer finally took Carol from us, the little glass piano still occupies its place of honor there.

Parenting Strategy

Paul felt bad for his careless mistake and the unintended but real pain he caused his mother. He admitted his error, and his mother fully forgave him and held no grudge against him. So why did this incident linger in Paul's mind and continue to bother him, even years later? Part of a truly effective apology is demonstrating by your actions that you take responsibility. As Paul matured and grew in wisdom, understanding, and skill, he finished the apology he began so long ago by making amends.

Apologizing, like forgiveness, is a choice and a skill. Ask your child to think of someone whom she has hurt in some way. If your child is older, she may even make a list of multiple people. Then ask her to select one person and consider apologizing. Even if your child is not ready to apologize right now, tell her that you would like to teach her the basic steps of an apology so that she will know how to do it effectively when she is ready. Be patient; it's not helpful to push your child to apologize too quickly or under too much pressure.

Elements of an effective apology:

1. Clearly state how you hurt the other person and how you think the other person feels.
2. Take full responsibility for your choices and actions.
3. Tell the other person that you are sorry.
4. Tell the other person what you learned from the experience and the changes you are making so that you will not harm the other person this way again.
5. Tell the other person what you are planning to do to make amends. Ask if your planned action would cause any harm. If it would, adjust your plans accordingly. If not, follow through in a timely way, whether or not the other person forgives you.
6. Ask the other person to forgive you.

Just glancing over this review, it is clear that some of the elements are more critical than others. Taking responsibility and making amends are two of the most important. If your child says, "I'm sorry" without owning up to her actions or making any repair, it will likely seem pretty hollow. A lasting change of heart and behavior is often crucial to the other person's decision of whether or not to reconnect after forgiving.

Apologies can be made in many ways, depending on the circumstances. Apologizing in person is usually the most powerful, but there are times when that is not possible or even appropriate. An effective apology can be made in writing or even over the phone. Help your child consider what is best in each situation. Your child's resiliency will grow as she learns from her own mistakes, feels and expresses genuine sorrow, and makes lasting changes and meaningful repairs.

THE BLUE SWEATER: A CHOICE AND A SKILL

"The weak can never forgive. Forgiveness is the attribute of the strong."
Mahatma Gandhi

When your child is hurt, his first reaction may be anger. Anger can feel good, powerful, and even protective, at least for a while. If it goes on and on, however, it can destroy his sense of well-being. Other times, your child may react to hurt by feeling sad. Underneath both sadness and anger is pain. In the long run, your child's body, mind, and spirit suffer when he is stuck in anger, pain, or sadness. Forgiveness can make him whole again and help him develop the resiliency to move forward. Instead of wishing a negative experience had never happened, you can help your child choose to learn valuable life lessons. Choosing forgiveness gives him power over his own life; choosing resentment gives that power to others. Through practicing forgiveness, he can take charge and set his own course.

Cal's Story

The air was frigid, with that sharp, piercing chill that hurts when you try to breathe. The sidewalks were treacherous, slick sheets of pure ice, and I knew that if I was going to go for a walk that day, I should really walk indoors at the local gym. I started off around the track, wearing my favorite thick, warm blue sweater, but with each lap, I got hotter and hotter. I looked around, wondering what to do, and decided to lay my sweater down on the railing and continue my walk. Lost in thought, about 35 or 40 minutes later, I noticed my sweater was gone. My next observation, I have to admit, was that a young man who had been sitting near my sweater was gone, too. Not wanting to assume or accuse him of something he may or may not have done, I looked over the railing to see if it had fallen onto the bleachers. It hadn't. I continued to look around the gym, and even checked the lost and found. I never found it.

I don't really know what happened to my beautiful blue sweater, but I do know that I had a choice. I could choose to be upset, blame someone, and hold on to resentment, or I could choose to let it go. Of course, I realize that the loss of a sweater, even a favorite blue sweater, is a small loss in the bigger picture of life, but it turns out that how we handle small things creates the pattern for how we handle the bigger ones, which will surely come into all of our lives.

Parenting Strategy

Make it a habit to tell your child stories about the big and little things that are happening all around you or have happened in the past. Highlight how people respond to both positive and negative experiences. You might find inspiration in your own experiences, like Cal and his sweater, or in newspaper articles, political events, local happenings in your neighborhood or school, historical events, etc. Wherever there are people, there are stories.

Ask your child to tell you stories. As the stories unfold, talk about the possibilities for forgiving, apologizing, being forgiven, or reconnecting. Play out the different possible outcomes. Make it a regular practice. Help your child choose to not take offense or let another person's small-mindedness lead him to resentment. Your child will develop greater empathy, insight, and wisdom to inform good decisions about forgiveness and the resiliency to choose his own path in the face of challenges.

Chapter 5

SELF-WORTH

"Because one believes in oneself, one doesn't try to convince others. Because one is content with oneself, one doesn't need others' approval. Because one accepts oneself, the whole world accepts him or her."
Lao-Tzu

THE NEW GIRL: SEE LIFE THROUGH YOUR CHILD'S EYES

"Every word, facial expression, gesture, or action on the part of a parent gives the child some message about self-worth. It is sad that so many parents don't realize what messages they are sending."
Virginia Satir

At a recent conference we attended, Dr. Robert Brooks, PhD, said, "Something you say today may stick with a child for the rest of her life." Wow! Think about it. The way you speak and act with your child today may impact her life for years to come. When you read this, did your thoughts immediately go to, "It's reassuring to think that my kind and thoughtful words will stick with my child," or did your thoughts go to, "Oh, my gosh, I've already snapped at her twice today and said such harsh things! Is there any hope?" Or possibly, like most of us, you are somewhere in the middle. How you interact with your child day in and day out is as important, if not more so, than how you handle the big events of life. You shape your child's sense of her own self-worth by the patterns of your daily routines.

Anne's Story

It was one of those long, warm autumn afternoons. I was the "new girl" at school, again, and at the worst possible time: the beginning of junior high. We had moved three times in four years, and Mom and Dad, hoping to cheer me up, promised we would not move again. I, on the other hand, would have leaped at the chance to move anywhere, as long as I never had to show my face at that school again. Ah, to escape the horror of gym class and the dread of changing into my new blue gym suit in that locker room full of girls with no way to hide my bare, pancake-flat baby chest amid those proud, round, well-filled bras.

After gym came lunch, with its own special horrors. I walked alone among all those unknown kids calling to friends and saving places for them. "No, you can't sit there, that's saved for Nancy." I finally slipped in by the "losers" and distanced myself from them by pretending to be engrossed in my book, well aware that I was fooling no one, especially not myself. Hiding behind my glasses as hot tears pricked my eyes, I worked on my mask of indifference.

Imagine my surprise later that afternoon when I heard the doorbell ring and caught a glimpse of Stacy, the ruling eighth-grade queen of the neighborhood, standing on my porch with an envelope in hand. Timidly, hardly daring to hope, I crossed the room as if in a dream and opened the door. "Here, this is an invitation to my birthday party. My mother told me I had to give it to you, but don't you dare show up." With a flip of her perfect ponytail, she was gone, leaving me standing there, my shame and embarrassment exposed to all the world. I slipped the door shut and stood in shocked silence.

My mom came rushing up, so excited. "See, I knew you would make friends. When is the party?"

The words tumbled out of me: "No, there is no party for me. Don't you get it? She doesn't want me to come; her mother made her invite me."

"Oh, Anne, I'm sure you misunderstood. Of course she wants you to come."

I gave up trying to make Mom understand. I always gave up trying to make her understand. Now, don't get me wrong, my mother was a kind and caring person, but she just couldn't quite comprehend this shy, quiet late bloomer who was so different from herself and her other children.

As the fateful day approached, I earnestly pleaded to all the powers of heaven that Mom would forget the date or would somehow get distracted. No such luck. She attempted to persuade, cajole, or guilt me into going, never realizing I felt I was battling for my soul. I had replayed the scene a million times. I saw the smirk and knew the intention of the hurtful snub. I took a stand and claimed my voice through action. I would not go, not to comply with the insulting directive, but because I had seen through the queen's mask and did not want to be friends with someone who would treat anyone like that.

I wish I could say I used my voice to speak up confidently for myself and my values from that time forth, but that is not the truth. After years of experience, both painful and delightful, I can say with pride that my voice is stronger and that I know more of the sorrows and joys of life and relationships. I know the pain of struggling alone and the value of great mentors. I am learning to choose more wisely, nurture my relationships with care, and focus on being the kind of friend, spouse, mom, and grandma I aspire to be.

Parenting Strategy

Anne's mom truly was a loving and caring mother, and years after this experience she and Anne had some wonderful, healing conversations and learned much from and about each other. Anne's mom honestly wanted the best for her daughter and was just trying to be positive, not insensitive. But, as often happens, that day she missed an opportunity to connect with and support her daughter. Of all the things you will ever do to help your child develop a strong sense of her self-worth, just listening—really listening—and hearing what she has to say is the most important of all.

We know this can be hard in the busy hubbub of the day. It's so much easier to dismiss your child or let the moment slip by. The key is true empathy, really placing yourself in your child's shoes and trying to imagine what her experience is like for her. Research shows that it is important to hear both the content of what your child is trying to say and how she is feeling. When your child tells you something, check it out with her. Make sure you hear both the content and her feelings correctly.

GIRL WITH THE BRIGHT RED DRESS: SAFE AND CONNECTED

"Don't ask yourself what the world needs, ask yourself what makes you come alive. And then go and do that. Because what the world needs is people who have come alive."
Howard Washington Thurman

All children have an inborn drive to try new things and develop their sense of mastery. Do you remember watching your child try and try and try again to roll over, sit up, crawl, and walk?

When children are nurtured in an emotionally safe and positive environment, they remain open to growing and changing. They explore and experiment in safety, knowing that they are not being judged by whether they succeed but rather are being supported and cherished as they figure out what they can do, who they are, and what they value. Conversely, when children live in an emotionally negative or unsafe environment, they tend to protect themselves from potential harm by shutting down and being less open to change and growth.

Cal's Story

Some time ago, I attended church with my wife, one of her sisters, and her sister's family. While sitting in the chapel listening to the speaker, I noticed that in the pew directly in front of me there was a young couple with four children, three girls and one boy. I was impressed by how this couple was teaching their young family how to be reverent.

The youngest was a little girl, whom I judged to be about nine or ten months old, and loved to wiggle, squirm, and stand up holding onto the bench with her tiny little hands. She was wearing a bright red dress, a red headband with silver stars, and a binky that seemed to be glued to her mouth. This rambunctious little angel was full of energy as she bounced back and forth between her mom and dad, who were sitting about two or three feet apart, trying to pay attention to the speaker. I was fascinated watching her as she stood up and sat down, then up, then down, as though she were using the back of the bench to play peekaboo with me. Every now and then when she poked her head up, she would look at me to see if I was watching her and then would grab a couple of my fingers, which I had teasingly placed where she could find them.

It didn't take very long for this little sweetheart to capture my heart. I loved watching her just being a little girl, but what really caught my attention was her mother. I studied this young mother's reaction. She was not frustrated with her daughter. It seemed she understood that in her daughter's wanderings on that church bench, she was exploring an aspect of living in the here and now. I marveled at the patience and kindness she showed her little daughter. After all, more advanced lessons in church etiquette could wait for some future day.

Watching this interaction, the thought crossed my mind that, in a few years, if this mother shows her daughter this same kind of patience and kindness when she is a teenager, a positive relationship will permeate their home. Someday this girl and her siblings will love to come back home, visit with their family, and bring their children with them to experience the joy of being with their beloved Grandma and Grandpa.

Parenting Strategy

The couple in Cal's story appears to be well on their way to making their family a safe haven in which their children can thrive. Your child, like all children, is most likely to develop those traits he sees modeled in his home. You can help him develop a healthy sense of his own worth by developing the kind of qualities that help people feel safe and connected. Do you want your child to be patient? Kind? Respectful? Put deliberate time and effort into being more patient, kind, and respectful to yourself and others, including your child.

What do you say about yourself when you face a challenge, make a mistake, or hurt someone's feelings? What do you say about others, your friends, neighbors, coworkers, or child when they do something irritating or disappointing? Model being accurate, truthful, and caring. For example, if you forget to do something, instead of saying, "Oh, I'm so stupid!" try saying something like, "I meant to remember that. I guess I'll think of a way to remind myself so I can do better next time." You will be demonstrating both self-respect and the resiliency to learn from your mistakes.

Do the same when speaking of others. One of the best ways to teach your children to be *disrespectful* is to speak negatively about others. The same principle applies to your child. If you are respectful when you speak to and about him, you will be well on your way to making your family a safe haven in which he can thrive.

THE LEOPARD'S STRENGTH: WELL-ROUNDED ACCEPTANCE

"Self-pity gets you nowhere. One must have the adventurous daring to accept oneself as a bundle of possibilities and undertake the most interesting game in the world—making the most of one's best."
Harry Emerson Fosdick

To nurture a sense of self-worth, your child needs you, as her parent, and other trusted adults to notice her and talk about all of her attributes. An honest and loving yet well-rounded acceptance of your child's whole self is vital to building trust, respect, and a deep sense of her own worth. Your child will trust you more and be more likely to catch a meaningful vision of her worth when you use accurate language to realistically acknowledge both her challenges and her strengths.

We once heard a story about an economist who gave a speech on how to keep a business profitable during a recession. At the beginning of her presentation, she put a large poster on an easel. All that was on the poster was a small black spot. She asked a businessman sitting in the front row what he saw, and the man promptly replied, "A black dot."

Then she methodically went around the room, asking the same question to all the attendees and receiving the same answer from each. After getting everyone's opinion, and with a deliberate and careful emphasis on her words, she said, "Yes, there is a small black dot, but I am surprised that no one said anything about all the white space on the poster. The white space represents business potential that you all overlooked." With that, she concluded her talk and sat down.

What do you see when you look at your child? Do you mostly see the small black dot, or do you mostly see all the white space that represents her potential? Can you see her as a whole, both the dot and the potential, complete and together?

Cal's Story

In the genus *Panthera*, there are four big cats: the tiger, the lion, the jaguar, and the leopard. Of these four, the leopard has the distinction of being the smallest, yet his seeming limitation is a strength he can use to survive. Due to his smaller size, he is not as powerful as his cousins, but he sure can hide and lunge from small spaces into which they will never be able to squeeze! He is who he is, and he survives the world of the jungle by doing what he does best.

I have Tourette syndrome (TS), a neuropsychological condition I cannot change any more than the leopard can grow to be the same size as his cousins. I could moan about my challenges or focus on what I don't have and be miserable, but I am grateful that as a youngster, my parents taught me to live and thrive with who I am.

If you watch a video of me on our website, www.ResilientChild. com, you will see how my eyes screw up and kind of roll around all over my face, my mouth twitches, my shoulders jerk. These are Tourettic tics, involuntary muscle movements. You may have heard that people with TS swear or call out obscenities all the time. That is called *coprolalia*, which some people with TS do have, but I don't—so if you hear me swear, you will know that I meant it!

I get painful muscle knots from some of my Tourettic tics, especially the ones in my neck. Tics also make it difficult for me to do some of the things I want to do. For example, imagine how hard it would be to read a book, let alone write one, if every 10 to 15 seconds you had to stop, flap your hands up and down, pull a funny face, blink five times, and then stand up and sit back down. Try timing yourself writing something simple like the Pledge of Allegiance as you would normally do it, and then try it again, giving yourself the same amount of time but adding in the little routine above every 10 to 15 seconds. How far did you get the second time? That gives you a window into some of my challenges.

On the other hand, I believe that having TS has pushed me to develop my sense of humor, to accept others and their challenges, and to be more kind and thoughtful. It has taught me patience and perseverance. It has shaped my values and helped me set my priorities. People have asked me if I would give up having TS if I could, but that has always seemed like kind of a crazy question to me, because I can't. For me, the key to living with TS is to be like the leopard: to accept who I am and to recognize, appreciate, and use the skills and talents I do have in order to thrive in my personal jungle.

How is it for you and your child? How do you help her appreciate and be content with who she is? As parents, we have an obligation to help our children find ways to live full, productive lives with whatever challenges they may have.

Parenting Strategy

Notice your child's full potential rather than focusing too much on her black dot or seeming limitations. Every child has challenges, all of which can be great strengths as well. So, step out into the figurative jungle and help her develop with pride and confidence.

Think deeply and accurately about your child. Take one full minute to really see her in your mind's eye. Notice what she looks like, how tall she is, the color of her hair, eyes, and skin, the way she smiles and frowns. Hear her voice in your head when she is happy, sad, or angry. Remember the way she smells when you hug her tight or kiss her goodnight. Think about her strengths and weaknesses. Just lately, have you been paying more attention to her potential or to her flaws?

Try to see the whole picture of who she is more clearly. How could this begin to change how she sees herself and feels about herself? How could this impact her courage, her sense of self-worth, her willingness to take a risk, to stretch and grow?

The human brain has a natural negativity bias; it notices problems and errors much more quickly and remembers them more easily than it does positive experiences. To feel loved and secure in her relationship with you, your child needs at least five positive interactions with you to every negative one. When you are tempted to focus on the negative, pause and ask yourself, "How is my relationship bank account? Am I making enough positive deposits?" Be accurate, truthful, and lovingly supportive.

THE SMILE THAT CAPTURED MY HEART: SERVE OTHERS

"If only you could sense how important you are to the lives of those you meet; how important you can be to people you may never even dream of. There is something of yourself that you leave at every meeting with another person."
Fred Rogers

The surest path to feeling a deep sense of self-worth and contentment with life is to find our greatest strengths and use them to serve others and make the world a better place. What are your child's signature strengths? How can you help him find ways to use his talents in the service of others and improve the world around him?

Cal's Story

I sat in church this morning, anticipating a beautiful service. I was excited to hear the children as they put on their annual program. Traditionally, this consists of the children's chorus singing the songs they've learned that year, as well as each child sharing a small speaking part.

Vivienne was a four-year-old Chinese girl who had recently been adopted by a loving family in our congregation. She did not speak much English yet and was trying to adjust to a new culture and way of life. As she sat in the front row, I watched her closely and noticed that she always had a smile on her face. It didn't take me long to realize how contagious her smile was. I could not take my eyes off this little girl as she stood there, singing and smiling to the congregation. Occasionally, she would mimic the chorister and move her arms as though she was leading the music.

I was sitting close enough that I could hear what she was singing. Sometimes I heard English words, and other times I couldn't recognize what language she was singing in. In reality, it didn't matter, because she was enjoying herself as she sang with vigor and smiles. Every now and then, I heard her sing a simple English word that I knew she had learned in her home. "Family," "love," and "me" rang out with gusto. Several times, she turned to look and smile at her older brother and two older sisters. They smiled back, letting her know that they loved her and were proud of her.

I not only saw the enjoyment in Vivienne's eyes, but I also felt the love she had for her family. Most importantly, I felt a special spirit emanating from this precious, beautiful, innocent little girl. Her sweet spirit touched the hearts of many in the congregation. I saw her smile warm their hearts and inspire them to smile back at her with real, vibrant smiles, just like hers.

Parenting Strategy

Vivienne's family helped build her sense of worth by encouraging her to stand tall, sing out with the choir, and do her best, even when she didn't know all of the words. They could have tried to shield her from making mistakes, gotten upset when she sang the wrong words, or discouraged her from joining with the other children. She had good reason to be shy or feel awkward, but her parents could see that, in spite of her challenges, Vivienne also had great strengths to share. Her joyful enthusiasm and contagious smile brightened the day for everyone in attendance. Vivienne's resiliency grew that day as she shared her talents, served her community, and made it a better place.

Watch your child. Notice his strengths. Look deeper than whether he's good at hitting a ball or playing the piano. Look at his inner strengths, those qualities that make him special. Is he kind or thoughtful, quick to observe and respond to the needs of his little brother, the dog, or the lonely neighbor? Is he playful, good-natured, the one who organizes a game, tells a joke, and gets everyone laughing? Is he hard-working, conscientious, dutiful, the one who notices when something needs to be repaired or put away and gets right on it? Is he patient, gentle, the one who waits for others and doesn't rush them or make them feel hurried or pressured?

Make it a point to give your child one sincere compliment each day that includes a quality you notice in him and a little story about how you saw that quality demonstrated in his words or actions. Help him see how he uses his strengths to serve others or make the world a better place. For example, "I noticed how thoughtful you were with your friend whose dad lost his job. I thought you were sensitive and generous in the way you suggested you could work together to organize a neighborhood garage sale to earn money for the scout trip this summer."

Now you try one. Think of something you've noticed your child say or do recently that demonstrated one of his inner qualities or strengths and how he served others or made the world a better place in some small way. Rehearse in your mind how you could tell him the story. Sharing the story makes the compliment much more meaningful. Now go tell him! And then repeat. If you do it every day for 27 days, you will have made a new habit.

A MOTHER'S BELIEF: SUPERVISED RISK

"I've learned that fear limits you and your vision. It serves as blinders to what may be just a few steps down the road for you. The journey is valuable, but believing in your talents, your abilities, and your self-worth can empower you to walk down an even brighter path. Transforming fear into freedom—how great is that?"
Soledad O'Brien

Fear paralyzes many children, and oftentimes a child's fears have at least some basis in reality. If your child stood up in front of the class to give a report, she might make an embarrassing mistake. If she played a piano solo, she might forget her piece in the middle of her performance. If she tried out for the basketball team, she might not get picked. If she did make the team, she might miss a free throw shot and dash her team's chance to go to the finals. All of these potential failures could also be opportunities for growth. Your child might have success, gain the respect of others, make new connections, feel more a part of her community, or even have the chance to learn and grow from a setback.

What happens between you and your child when she wants to do things that might cause her to struggle, or even fail? Do you encourage and support her, or try to protect her? When she is afraid to take risks, do you encourage her to play it safe, or do you help her look at all the possibilities and let her know you think she is amazing just for being willing to try and learn from whatever happens?

Cal's Story

In the spring of 2016, I spoke at the national conference of the Tourette Association of America, held in Washington, D.C. After my presentation, I asked for comments or questions. A young mother named Kirsten raised her hand and described an experience with her son Henry that had taken place two days earlier.

Henry had Tourette syndrome (TS), which, as previously explained, is a neuropsychological disorder characterized by involuntary muscle movements known as tics. He had also been diagnosed with high-functioning autism. This young man was 13 years old and had been invited to give a three-minute speech at a Congressional Luncheon on Capitol Hill. His assigned topic was to describe what it is like to live with TS.

The night before the luncheon, Henry's mother suggested that he practice his talk, thinking it would help build his confidence. He agreed, but as he began practicing, his stuttering tic went into full force mode, and he struggled mightily, hardly able to get a word out. Finally, he just gave up and "shut down." His confidence disappeared, and he told his mother he couldn't do it. His wise mother gave him a tender hug, suggested he get some sleep, and said she would help him practice in the morning.

After getting up and getting ready for the day, Kirsten said, "You know something, Henry? Today is going to be an amazing day, because you have a great opportunity to speak to members of Congress and tell them your story about living with adversity. I know that you have practiced and prepared and will do very well."

She was positive with him as she encouraged, supported, and helped him regain his confidence. She helped him recapture his belief that he could do it, and then, with a mother's love, she reminded him that she would be standing on the stage with him. She assured him that, if necessary, she would finish his talk for him, but only if Henry complied with one condition: first, he must try.

When it was time for Henry to speak, Kirsten stood next to her son, showing him that she believed in him but was also ready to help if needed. He bravely stood in front of this large group of people, looked into the faces of the congressional representatives who were in attendance to hear him, and then started to speak. An amazing thing happened to Henry at that moment: he experienced another full-blown episode of his stuttering tic, but with his renewed confidence, he kept going and finished his talk. The courage he showed was visible to all who were there, and they rewarded him with a rousing standing ovation.

His mother's actions were also courageous. No parent wants their child to fail, and any parent in this situation would worry. This mother patiently helped Henry prepare and then stood beside him to support him if he needed her.

Parenting Strategy

Supervised risk-taking is an important part of building a child's sense of self-worth. Every child—yours included—has both strengths and challenges. Some challenges are quite obvious, like some of Henry's; others are more subtle. Each child has a choice: do I spend my life upset about the things I cannot change, or focus on the things I can do? This choice is an important part of helping your child develop a sense of self-worth and feeling empowered in life. Start with everyday events. What does your child complain about? How she looks? What she is having for dinner? Doing chores? Her test scores? Not having the newest video game or the fanciest cell phone? Family rules? Homework? Friends?

Help your child change the direction of her thoughts. First, ask her if what she is complaining about is something she can change or not. If not, help her learn how she can accept and live with what she doesn't like. Henry, for instance, cannot change that he has TS and is learning to accept and live with the challenges that go along with it. Even though Henry has TS and will always have TS, there are many aspects of his life that he can change. He can change how he copes with TS, choose whether he gives a speech or not, pick which opportunities he takes on or passes up, and decide which of his talents he wants to develop.

If your child complains about things that can be changed, help her decide whether or not she is willing to work towards change. If your child is willing to work towards change, help her set small, realistic goals to get started moving in the direction she would like to go. If she doesn't like what you have for dinner, does she want to learn how to cook and help make different meals? If she wants a new game or device, is she willing to earn the money to buy it, and does she have ideas about how she can earn money?

How we do small things helps us become more confident in approaching the bigger issues of life and facing these challenges. Always praise your child for her effort, personal growth, and progress, not for reaching some objective standard of achievement. Sometimes your child's action will be a great success; other times she may falter or even fail. When a project doesn't go as planned, help her figure out what she can learn from her experience and see that failure is not something to be feared but an opportunity to learn. By encouraging your child to step up to small challenges, you will prepare her to take bigger risks, confident in the knowledge that you value her and will stand by her, and that she can value herself, regardless of the outcome. This is how resiliency grows.

Chapter 6

HUMOR

"Start every day off with a smile and get it over with."
W. C. Fields

MISS MILLS'S CLOSET: HOW TO SHARE A GOOD LAUGH

"The most wasted of all days is one without laughter."
e. e. cummings

Humor is truly a basic human quality and is routinely listed as one of the most vital resiliency skills. Infants smile their first real smile somewhere between just six and twelve weeks of age. They catch your eye, their eyes light up, and they smile over and over again, joyfully connecting with those around them. Through smiles, they express their feelings and engage with others. Around three to four months of age, babies take the next big step and begin to laugh out loud. They throw out their arms and kick their feet, their little bodies squirming with fun and fully joining in the celebration.

Humor is contagious. As you help your child develop her sense of humor, she will begin to appreciate how humor can connect her with people in many positive ways. When we laugh, we open our hearts. We let down our defenses and become more vulnerable.

We transform ordinary moments into extraordinary memories. Sharing a joke, a funny story, a giggle, or a good belly laugh helps us experience our common humanity.

A sense of humor is something that all of us can develop. Without a doubt, Cal is known for his great sense of humor, but he says that wasn't always the case. When he was much younger, he didn't feel very comfortable using humor. Once he started experimenting with it, however, he quickly realized its amazing potential. He often says that his sense of humor has gotten him into and out of a lot of trouble in his life, but that, fortunately, it has gotten him out of more trouble than it has gotten him into!

Cal's Story

Miss Mills was my fourth-grade teacher. She was young, attractive, athletic, fun to be with, and, though a strict disciplinarian, she was still everyone's favorite teacher. She knew that fourth-grade students acted like fourth-grade students, and she expected nothing more and nothing less. We knew all the rules—the class rules, the playground rules, and the school rules—and we knew she would hold us to them. Part of her physical education schedule included dancing, and when the boys put up a fuss, she didn't listen. We knew that if we didn't find a partner, she would assign us one, and, for whatever reason, none of us wanted that!

The memory of one event that year is seared into my brain and became a legend in my family. What I did was impulsive, brave, crazy, and should probably be classified as just plain stupid. It all started one beautiful spring afternoon. We had just come back from recess, and, like everyone else, I was feeling energetic and relaxed. I got back to class before Miss Mills and took my seat in the front row, close to the storage closet where she kept the playground equipment.

That afternoon, Miss Mills came in from recess carrying the equipment and went directly to the closet to put it away. I can still see her clearly as she walked into the closet and bent over, with her back towards me, to put the equipment in its place. I was just sitting there, minding my own business, with no evil intent or desire, when out of the blue, just like that, an idea popped into my head. In no time at all, I calculated the distance from my desk to the closet and decided that I could run to the closet, slam the door shut on her, and get back to my seat without her knowing who did it.

It turns out my calculations were *almost* accurate. I jumped out of my seat, ran to the closet, slammed the door on my teacher, and was back in my seat before she came out. Unfortunately— or fortunately, depending on how you look at it—I did not get away with my dastardly deed. I was promptly kicked out of class and spent the rest of the afternoon leaning against the wall in the hallway. I was surprised that she caught me, and it wasn't until years later that I realized that teachers are trained to protect their backs. She did a great job!

A few days later, I saw Miss Mills walking near my house. She didn't live in my neighborhood, and I had the sinking feeling that she was heading towards my house, so I did the brave thing and ran. Sure enough, she went right up to my front door and then disappeared inside to have a talk with my mother. I was quite certain that when I got home from running away, I was, as kids used to say, "going to get it" from my mom. What actually happened is an example of why Miss Mills was such an excellent teacher. After visiting with Mom and explaining about the closet incident, she made a suggestion, which my mom wisely followed.

Miss Mills suggested that my mom go light on the punishment (for which I was grateful) because she had already dispensed it and felt I had learned an important lesson. She also confessed to Mom that she had to stay in the closet for a few extra moments that day until she could get her own laughter under control. I'm sure that, like my family, she has had fun telling this story many times throughout her life.

Parenting Strategy

Encourage your child's sense of humor, laugh with her at her sometimes impulsive actions, create lasting memories of fun, and still hold her accountable for keeping her behavior in appropriate bounds. As her sense of humor develops, she will become more confident and better able to cope effectively with daily life as well as the challenges and stresses that come her way. Teach your child to seek out the Miss Millses of the world: strong, capable people who combine honor, sensitivity, and humor.

If your child does not yet have a very well-developed sense of humor, start with small, simple steps. The most natural place to start is with smiling. The simple act of smiling can put people in a different emotional state. How often do you see your child smile? How often do you smile at her, really smile, all the way down to your toes, like a baby? If you are both off to a good start here, enrich it and make it stronger. Either way, make a conscious choice to catch your child's eyes with yours, let your love shine through to her, and let your eyes sparkle with delight to see her. Let your eyes scrunch a bit and your face light up. This is how you begin to gather her in and connect.

The next step is simple, repeat, repeat, repeat. Smiling is literally contagious. If you start smiling and keep smiling over and over again—playfully, invitingly, sincerely wanting just to share the moment—you will be irresistible.

Once you are sharing smiles regularly, have some fun with it. You've probably had a staring contest before, right? How about a smiling contest? Face off, playfully look into each other's eyes, and see who can hold their smile the longest without breaking away. At our house, that usually ends in giggles, if not uproarious laughter. A frowning contest usually ends just the same way, too!

THE FROG IN THE MILK BUCKET: RELAX AND ENJOY

"A sense of humor...is needed armor. Joy in one's heart and some laughter on one's lips is a sign that the person down deep has a pretty good grasp of life."
Hugh Sidey

Do you ever feel like your family life has become one long grind of do this, don't do that? "Do your chores." "Did you finish your homework?" "Stop hitting your brother." Maybe it's time to get off the treadmill and add more fun to your life.

There are huge benefits to having fun and a good laugh. Laughter helps you open up and connect with other people. It relaxes your body, gives your immune system a boost, releases endorphins (those naturally occurring "feel good" hormones), and even protects your heart. When you laugh and have fun regularly, you are less adversely affected by stress and better able to maintain a sense of well-being, even in the face of difficult situations.

Cal's Story

One afternoon, two brothers had some extra time before they had to help their father with the milking, so they decided to play at a nearby pond. While playing, the boys became fascinated with a frog that was enjoying the day, jumping around the edges of the pond. Every now and then, the frog would notice a fly or some other bug trying to sneak by it. More quickly than the eye could see, his tongue would whip out and catch these bugs for his afternoon snack. As the brothers watched the frog feed himself, they hatched a plan to catch it and play a marvelous joke on their father. It wasn't easy to catch him, but after several attempts, they succeeded and hurried to the barn to have some fun with their father.

They quickly settled into their chores, and when the milking was nearly done, they snuck the frog into the bucket of fresh milk their father used to feed a calf. They were excited to see their father's face when he found the frog swimming in that bucket of milk. Unfortunately for them, their father had already fed the calf, so their well-planned surprise didn't happen. They finished up their chores and went to the house for supper, completely forgetting about the frog and the bucket of milk.

Later that night, one of the boys woke up and remembered the frog. He woke his brother to discuss what they should do, but they decided they couldn't do anything until morning. They surprised their dad when they showed up at the barn early the next morning. Before the boys could take care of the frog, their dad picked up the bucket and called to his sons to come see what was inside. Trying to act cool, they were stunned when they looked inside and saw that the frog and the milk were gone, but the bucket wasn't empty—it was full of butter. Confused, the boys told their dad what had happened, and he let out a big belly laugh, which calmed the boys, and they laughed with him. Then he used the moment to teach a great lesson.

"Well," he said to his sons, "that frog was one of those energized, undefeatable type frogs. He wouldn't give up and let you enjoy the surprise on my face, so he swam all night and churned the milk into butter, and then he jumped out and hurried home to tell his family about his great adventure."

Parenting Strategy

Listen to your child and take advantage of the moment to have some fun and even sneak in a lesson once in a while. Show your child that you can go along with a good-natured joke without taking offense. When you share moments that involve humor, your child will both see and feel your playful side, and the bond between you will be strengthened. Letting your child see your fun side and separating it from your serious self will be good for him and for you as well. It will help both of you to not take yourselves too seriously. When you laugh at your own weaknesses, and even mistakes, you help your child learn to do the same, which is a great resiliency skill!

I'LL STEP ON YOUR TOE AND CALL YOU A DUMB-DUMB!: THE ART OF NOT TAKING YOURSELF TOO SERIOUSLY

"Laughter is the closest distance between two people."
Victor Borge

There are, of course, times when the use of humor would be offensive or inappropriate. There are other times when it is just the thing to help someone face even a difficult challenge with resiliency. Many years ago, Cal went with his first wife, Carol, to the hospital to visit a friend who was dying from a rare form of lung cancer. Gerald knew his condition was terminal and was preparing himself and his family for that day when he would soon be gone.

That night, something magical happened. Cal started cracking jokes and telling stories about the crazy things he and his friend had done. Before long, the room was filled with laughter, and Cal's friend, lying in a hospital bed with only weeks to live, was laughing the hardest and the loudest of them all. After about 30 minutes, Cal could see that Gerald was getting tired, and he knew it was time to leave. As Cal and Carol were leaving, Gerald's wife walked out with them and thanked him. "It was good," she said, "that you were comfortable using humor with Gerald, because it cheered him up and gave him a few moments of respite where he didn't think about his condition."

When used with thoughtful sensitivity, humor can help us connect with others and get through the toughest of challenges. While that experience was many years ago, Cal still remembers with warmth and happiness the feelings of love shared in that hospital room that night as they all laughed and enjoyed their time together.

Anne's Story

My family purchased a lovely old home, built in 1924, on a beautiful tree-lined street in Salt Lake City. The house shared a long, narrow driveway with our next-door neighbors. In the spirit of cooperation, both families were careful not to block each other's garage or leave their cars in the driveway for more than a few minutes. Over the years, that driveway brought our family and the neighbors together. It provided us with frequent interactions as we met each other there, exchanged smiles, and called out "Good morning," "Howdy," and "How are you?" throughout the day. These chance meetings led to sharing humor, frustrations, happy events, and sad ones.

One hot summer day, my mom, the busy mother of a large family, committed the cardinal sin: she forgot to move the car after unloading her ten thousand bags of groceries. Meanwhile, five-year-old Steven, the cute and charming but determined youngest child who lived next door, waited and waited for an eternity, perhaps five minutes, expecting her to come back and move the car. He wanted to play and the car was in his way. His suffering was immense as he waited, frustration mounting.

Finally, he couldn't take it any longer. He boldly marched right up to our front door and knocked loudly. When Mom answered the door, Steven proceeded to chew her out using his best five-year-old vocabulary. As his indignation reached its peak, he pulled himself up to his tallest height, placed his hands menacingly on his hips, glared at Mom with the most ominous eyes he could muster, and threw out his ultimate threat: "I'm going to step on your toe and call you a dumb-dumb!" Mom, barely able to mask her laughter, graciously apologized and moved the car.

For years afterwards, this incident was a favorite family story. The phrase "I'm going to step on your toe and call you a dumb-dumb," along with a good imitation of Steven's hands on his hips and ominous glare with a bit of an added twinkle in the eye, became a beloved family expression when anyone started to feel frustrated with somebody. This simple phrase, delivered with just the right amount of humor, helped everyone keep life in perspective and defused many awkward situations with the inevitable smiles, laughter, and much needed softening of hearts that it created.

Parenting Strategy

All families have moments when disagreements can escalate into anger and hurt. A playful tradition like this one in Anne's family de-escalates disagreements and provides opportunities to laugh and enjoy the humorous side of distress. Humor is a great de-escalation method that you can develop and use to help your child cope with the inevitable frustrations of life. You can share this story with your own child, or one from your own experiences, and start a new family tradition. Be playful and sensitive, and, above all, have fun together with this. You and your child will learn to keep life events in perspective and not to take yourselves too seriously, which are marvelous skills for strengthening resiliency in the face of big and little challenges.

THAT DOG IS A THIEF!: THE FINE LINE BETWEEN PAIN AND LAUGHTER

"Humor is tragedy plus time."
Mark Twain

Humor can bring welcome relief by helping you change your perspective about otherwise distressing situations. Throughout time, humans have used humor to come to terms with difficult and even tragic situations. There is a fine line between what is funny and what is potentially offensive, and that line may be different for everyone. If an event is especially horrific or very recent, people are less likely to find humor in references to it; the less intense the event was and the longer it has been since it happened, the more likely we are to see the humor in it.

Finding the humor in our everyday challenges is a resilient way of accepting and moving forward from them. When Anne was growing up, her dad was a great listener—sensitive, open, and caring—yet, when something would go wrong, her dad would often find the right time to say, "So, did anyone get killed? Did anyone get scarred for life or permanently maimed? If not, then it's going to make a great story someday!" With that shift in perspective, he could usually help his kids find the humor in situations much sooner than later. Seeing the humor and starting to laugh disrupted the negative emotional response and provided a much-needed emotional release.

Our Story

On a beautiful fall day a few years ago, we had some business in downtown Salt Lake. On our lunch break, we decided we had just enough time to walk up City Creek Canyon for a quick picnic. We bought a couple of sandwiches and walked up the canyon, searching for a picnic table where we could sit quietly, enjoy the scenery, and just relax together.

We walked along, laughing and being silly, until we found the perfect spot. Leisurely, we sat down and unwrapped our delicious sandwiches, eagerly anticipating our first bite. That's when it happened. We didn't hear it coming; we didn't see it either. With no warning at all, a full-grown German Shepherd came running full tilt down the dirt trail, leaped towards Anne, and, in a single motion, grabbed her sandwich in its mouth and swallowed it whole, hardly breaking its stride as it careened off down the canyon. We sat there in shock.

We looked up the trail to see a young woman carrying a leash and running a short distance behind the dog, clearly its owner. Her big smile and loud chuckle let us know she had seen what had happened and thought her dog's actions were funny. She seemed to be enjoying the moment as she ran past without a word of apology or an offer to buy another sandwich.

We sat there for a moment, stunned, hardly believing what had just happened. The insult of the owner's insensitive attitude was even more annoying than the dog's behavior. Disbelief turned to anger, but, after a few minutes of dwelling on how rude and inconsiderate some people are, we looked at each other and burst out laughing. When we stepped back from our outrage, it was just too funny not to enjoy the humor of the moment.

Years later, we still occasionally recall the incident, shake our heads, and laugh nearly as hard as we did then. We still think the woman was rude and insensitive, but we don't let it bother us. We will never know why she didn't stop and talk to us, but we enjoy having a good laugh and a great story to share.

P.S. And at least we still had one sandwich to share for lunch!

Parenting Strategy

Above all, teach your child to be considerate, aware of her actions, and mindful of the consequences she may have on others. Help her think ahead and prevent hurt feelings whenever possible. Prevention is so much easier than repair.

Since not everyone will show your child the same kind of consideration, she will undoubtedly experience pain at times, so prepare her for that, too. Sensitively, help her learn to shift her perspective when appropriate by finding the humor in mildly distressing situations.

Start with yourself and set an example of using humor to change your perspective on some events in your life. How do you usually respond when things go wrong? Instead of moaning and groaning about the little frustrations of life, lightheartedly take your experience to the extreme—tell your child the story as if it were an old Seinfeld episode or a Saturday Night Live skit. As Anne's dad used to say, "It's going to make a great story someday," so why not start today to model making that shift with the little annoyances and troubles in your life? The woman at the checkout counter with a thousand coupons, the neighbor who borrows your edger and "forgets" to return it, and the clerk who messes up your order all present perfect opportunities. Now encourage your child to try it with one of her experiences. Often, taking it to the extreme will allow her mind to find the humor in otherwise frustrating or difficult daily experiences.

It was Anne's dad's playfulness and loving kindness that made it possible for him to help his children see the funny side of their pains. This is not about mocking or making light of your child's pain or struggles. First, clearly acknowledge your child's hurt, surprise, or other difficult emotion, then, at the right time and with insight and sensitivity, help her laugh with you at the craziness of life. As you do so, you and your child will become less critical of others, and even of yourselves. Teaching your child to find the humor in life and laughing together will draw you closer as a family and help her respond more flexibly and resiliently, no matter what challenges she faces.

HYRUM'S PRACTICAL JOKE: LAUGHTER BRINGS US CLOSER

"One of the things that binds us as a family is a shared sense of humor."
Ralph Fiennes

The effective use of humor demonstrates a form of emotional intelligence, an important part of your child's development and her ability to cope with life's ups and downs. Using humor well requires the ability to accurately read social situations, whether the humor is addressed to one person or a much larger audience, such as speaking to a group or even writing a Facebook post.

Emotional intelligence also informs the choice of the type of humor used. There are many different, delightful flavors of humor that can be appropriate. Other flavors are never a good choice, such as spiteful or demeaning jokes, smart-aleck or attention-seeking behaviors, poking fun at others in a hurtful way, damaging another's dignity or reputation, or rude challenges to authority, to name a few.

Cal remembers very clearly how he started to connect humor and emotional intelligence. It all started with an awkward situation that occurred one hot summer day while he was working with his uncle and grandfather, stacking hay. He was about 11 years old, and the stack was approximately 15 feet high. His job was to pick up a bale of hay and move it to the part of the stack where it was needed. He distinctly remembers walking to the edge of the stack to pick up a bale of hay when someone yelled at him, "Don't get so close to the edge, or you will fall," to which his uncle promptly responded, "Don't worry about Calvert because he takes one step forward and two steps backwards."

This comment drew lots of laughs, and Cal knew he had a choice to make. He could choose to be offended and sulk or to laugh and enjoy the moment. Either way, it was his decision. He remembers choosing to laugh freely with an open heart, as loud and hard as anyone. He knew that his uncle would never hurt him by making fun of him and that his uncle had a quick wit and used his humor to make the hot, miserable work fun. Neither Cal nor his uncle realized that day on top of the haystack that he was experiencing early symptoms of undiagnosed Tourette syndrome (TS) and comorbid obsessive-compulsive disorder (OCD).

One of the OCD symptoms that bothered him the most right then involved walking. If he stepped on something while walking, he felt compelled to go back, find whatever it was that he had stepped on, and keep stepping on it until it "felt right." It was as mystifying and frustrating to him as it was to whomever he was with. It took him forever to reach his destination. It was this behavior that triggered his uncle's comment and what made the incident so funny.

On the haystack that day, Cal learned that, by not taking offense and being able to laugh at himself along with his family, he could keep working with them and enjoy the day together. He learned to see the humor in his own actions and laugh *with* others. Perhaps most importantly of all, he learned that no one can hurt his feelings unless he lets them.

Cal's Story

While Anne and I were visiting one of our sons and his family in Germany, we decided to take a short trip to visit a few nearby sights. Now it may help you to get a better picture of our adventure to know that this son of ours, Paul, and his wife have eight children. We all piled into their 12-passenger van and headed out. Paul drove, and I sat towards the back with a bunch of the grandkids. We enjoyed a marvelous time together, eating yummy snacks, avoiding any "healthy" food, singing, telling stories, and listening to Grandma read a book out loud. We were having a great time together.

Hyrum, our eight-year-old grandson, always makes me feel good, and many times a day he says thoughtful things like, "Thanks for coming," or, "I love you, Grandpa." This cute, innocent little boy was sitting behind me and asked to see my watch. I put my left arm over the seat so he could "see it" and admire it, before he started to play with it. After a few minutes, he lost interest in the watch and turned his attention to something else.

We were having a wonderful time, but the drive went on and on. A missed turn here, a traffic jam there. It seemed like we would never get to our hotel. We finally arrived, late, tired, and barely able to crawl to our beds. I believe all of us were walking in our sleep as we entered our bedrooms. Several of us just fell on our beds without even taking off our shoes or brushing our teeth. I barely managed to set my watch alarm for 7:30, the agreed-upon time to set off again in the morning.

I awoke before the alarm went off and got up, but, after a few minutes, I crawled back into bed. My wife sleepily asked me the time, to which I responded, "6:30." The last thing I heard her say was, "Oh good! We still have an hour to sleep."

Not five minutes later, Paul knocked on our bedroom door and told us it was time to get up. "It's only 6:30, go back to bed," I yelled. He informed me that I was mistaken. It was 7:30, and I needed to get up right now or we would be late. At that moment, it dawned on me: my little buddy Hyrum had played a joke on me by setting my watch back an hour.

I suppose I could have gotten angry with Hyrum for almost making us late, but I knew he was on to me and my love of a good tease. All I could do was laugh at his joke and enjoy his humor. I couldn't even muster any fake anger to chew the little guy out. I had an epiphany that morning. I mean, I guess I had always known it, but it struck me with force that day. Life is meant to be fun, and incorporating laughter into it makes it all the more enjoyable.

At the breakfast table, I complimented Hyrum on pulling a good one on me and reminded him that he needed to be aware that I would get even with him when he least expected it. I noticed that his self-esteem went up with this good-natured, playful banter. It was going to be another great day!

Parenting Strategy

Weave fun and humor into the fabric of your everyday family life. Put up humorous posters, swap funny jokes, share clever sayings, or watch comedies together. Make it a habit to tell your child the funniest thing that happened to you or three funny things you noticed today. Invite her to do the same.

Be a model for your child of enriching your life by being playful yourself and spending time with fun, good-natured people. Encourage your child to notice that people with a well-developed sense of humor learn how far to go and when to stop. When she first tries using humor, she may make some mistakes or misread a situation. Patiently and with great kindness and care, help her see the other person's perspective, apologize, and make any needed repairs. As her sense of humor grows, she will deepen her understanding of others and her ability to read and respond accurately to their social cues.

Share your thoughts and experiences about how you choose when to use humor and when to hold back. Through shared trial and error, your child's sense of humor will grow. She will learn to think quickly, flexibly, and outside of the box. As she becomes more flexible in her thinking, she will come up with more creative solutions to problems and enhance her ability to respond well and adapt in the face of life's challenges, an essential resiliency skill. Enjoy watching your child's sense of humor grow and building fun memories together.

Chapter 7

Family Traditions

"Traditions have a very special way of keeping favorite memories forever in our hearts."
Unknown

CROSS-EYED BABY: CREATING WARMTH AND CONNECTION

"We didn't realize we were making memories; we just knew we were having fun."
Unknown

So many things are changing so fast these days that it can make your head swirl. Strong family traditions provide that solid sense of grounding and belonging your child needs to feel safe and secure in a changing world. The familiar, repeated pattern of traditions will help him develop the resiliency to successfully face his challenges today and all of the unknown ones his future will hold.

Some traditions are passed down from one generation to the next. There is something comforting about connecting across time this way. It helps your child know that he is part of something bigger than himself. Yet, it's important that traditions are also flexible enough to evolve along the way, adapting to the changing times and the unique individuals that make up families.

Cal's Story

When I was a young child, my grandfather would playfully scoop me up, put me on his knee, bounce me up and down, and sing:

> *Cross-eyed baby on each knee*
> *And a wife with a wart on her nose, on her nose,*
> *and a wife with a wart on her nose.*

I would laugh, savor the moment, and beg for more. Grandpa did this little activity with all of his grandchildren, and it was a great way for him to bond with us and let us know that he loved us and we were important to him.

When my children were young, I sang this little ditty to them, and now I sing it to my grandchildren and my first great-granddaughter. I was not blessed with my grandpa's beautiful singing voice, but it doesn't matter. When I sing this song to my family in my own crazy off-key way, they react the same way I did when I was their age, with the same smiles, laughter, and positive feelings.

I also notice that I benefit just as much, if not more, from this activity than my grandkids do. Singing this simple song while bouncing them on my knees creates a bonding moment. Simple connecting moments like this, repeated over and over, provide much of the pleasure of a richly lived life.

Whenever I put a child on my knees, bounce them, and sing, "Cross-eyed baby..." I feel the family connection flowing together, past, present, and future. Memories of my grandfather flood over me: his love, his voice, the time he spent with me, his example of fun, kindness, and appreciation for family. I see his legacy rolling forward as I watch my grandchildren's eyes and know they feel the love as well.

Parenting Strategy

Family traditions are meant to build warmth and safety. Effective ones are flexible enough to change with time and circumstances, while remaining constant enough to provide strong roots to ground our children through joy and pain. It doesn't matter whether Cal has a beautiful singing voice like his grandfather; Cross-Eyed Baby still binds the generations with playfulness and love.

Playfulness is an important quality to incorporate into family traditions. When you connect love with fun and laughter, your child stores away delightful experiences to support his resiliency and strengthen his ability to bounce forward when he is knocked back by the inevitable challenging and darker moments of life. He will know that there are good times and bad, and that he can move forward, expecting the good times to come around again.

Families are always changing through births, deaths, marriages, divorces, and other additions and separations, both long and short. Think of the traditions you already have and how your family is changing. Give yourself permission to *choose* which traditions to keep, to alter, to let go, to add. *Choose* to build strong, flexible traditions that help your family stay warm and strong. Your child will form deep, lasting memories of love and connection that he can fall back on when someone calls him names, he's left out of a group, or peers tempt him to join in a risky behavior. Challenges will come, and he will be ready.

THREE LITTLE KISSES: LASTING MEMORIES THROUGH DAILY RITUALS

"Listen earnestly to anything your children want to tell you, no matter what. If you don't listen eagerly to the little stuff when they are little, they won't tell you the big stuff when they are big, because to them all of it has always been big stuff."
Catherine M. Wallace

Small rituals, repeated daily, become a solid bedrock of resiliency to ground your child's connection to you and her family. Daily routines offer rich opportunities to create comforting, familiar patterns and expectations: how family members greet each other in the morning and when they return home, how they say goodbye, how they get ready for work, school, meals, and bed. Snack time, dance parties in the kitchen, bedtime stories, sharing highs and lows of the day while you and your child do the dishes or make the beds together, walks around the block—there are endless possibilities for all different ages and interests.

Positive daily rituals give a reliable structure to the day and something to look forward to through good times and bad. When your child is having fun with friends or a good day at school, these positive experiences will help her look forward to connecting with you and sharing her experiences. When she is having a rough time and her day is not going so well—maybe a new friend won't play anymore, she got a bad score on an assignment, or was dumped by a boyfriend or girlfriend—she will look forward to the comfort of knowing that you will be there to greet her when she gets home, and she will be able to count on the dependable daily routines of respect and connection you are building. She will have the resiliency to work through her challenges, with the solid support of daily rituals of connection.

When new challenges come along, having a deep reserve of daily connection from these routines will help your child hold on to a sense of herself as a dearly loved, well-understood, accepted, and respected human being. These lasting memories will help her have the resiliency to weather the storms of life, from losing a competition to losing a friend, or even losing confidence in herself for a while.

Cal's Story

For as long as I can remember, my parents had a daily ritual before Dad went to work and every evening when he came home. They gave each other three little kisses, and each little kiss represented one little word: I…Love…You!

My sisters and I noticed other expressions of love. Dad always treated Mom with gentleness and respect. He reached for her hand as they went out the door, praised her accomplishments, and quietly took on extra chores when he saw she was busy. We watched as he sought her opinion and listened to her advice. From his example, we learned to treat her with respect.

Mom showed her love and devotion to Dad by never disparaging him, supporting him as he worked long hours for meager pay, stretching the budget beyond what was expected of most wives and mothers, and encouraging him as he devoted long hours of volunteer service to their church. Together, they provided an anchor for each other based on their foundation of commitment and love. From this anchor, the family reaped the blessings of safety, connection, and freedom to be ourselves and know we are loved.

We witnessed those "three little kisses" day after day, year in and year out, and we felt their love for one another. Of course, they weren't perfect—no one is—but at the end of each day, whatever the ups and downs, they remembered that they loved and respected each other. When we were long gone from the home, raising families of our own, we knew that our parents still loved each other and still shared those little kisses every morning and every night. Even after 58 years of marriage, as Mom lay in a hospital bed set up in the dining room of their home, Dad leaned over the bed railing and asked for a kiss. She opened her eyes, found her strength, and puckered up just long enough to give him the last "three little kisses" they would share in this life.

The tradition of three little kisses lives on. I taught it to my first wife, Carol, and my children, then my wife Anne, and our grandchildren. Now our oldest grandson and his wife just brought home their first baby, and we are teaching it to her, too.

Parenting Strategy

All family traditions start sometime, so why not today? Positive little routines, repeated over and over, have tremendous power to shape your child's sense of family and security. There are many options, but the important thing is to actually pick one and put it into practice. A powerful start might be to create one new way of saying "I love you." It could be as simple as a fist bump, a touch on the shoulder, a special goodbye or hello, or even three little kisses. Talk to your child and let her know what it means to you.

Now, this next one is going to be tough for most of you, but I promise it will be of immense value. If you have any screens in your household (TVs, video games, tablets, cell phones, etc.), every day, for at least a few minutes, turn off all—repeat *all*—of them. Your child's screens, your screens, off. All of them. Spend some time face-to-face. Start with just a few minutes in the morning (if you are a morning person), afternoon, or evening. Gradually increase as your connection builds. Give her your undivided attention. Make space for secure attachment to flourish. Your child needs to connect with you as a caring, committed parent.

Many children today are overly connected to their friends, both in person and online. Friendships with peers are extremely important, but no matter how wonderful your child's friends are, they are also young people who lack the maturity and wisdom to truly understand, nurture, and protect your growing child, however young or old your child may be.

Maybe you will connect best in those precious moments right when your child gets home from school and is more likely to talk about her day; maybe it will be as you prepare, eat, or clean up after dinner. As much as humanly possible, eat at least one meal together every day, more if you can. Move sun and earth to make this happen. And make sure those meals are screen-free for all of you. Let your child know that she has 100% of your full and complete attention.

Whatever you choose, start today, start small, build up, and repeat daily. If you miss a day, start again the next day and keep going. Your child will come to feel seen, known, and understood with a deep and safe attachment. Make it a family tradition.

Consider the immense impact Cal's parents had with their repeated three little kisses. Those lasting memories of love and respect helped Cal develop the resiliency to face his challenges of having Tourette syndrome, obsessive-compulsive disorder, and attention deficit disorder. Simple little traditions provide many fond and happy memories, creating important anchors for your child now and throughout her life. You can build a reserve of memories through daily rituals in your family and provide your child with the resiliency that comes from the steady, predictable, and comforting patterns of safety and security.

SITTING AT GRANDMA'S FEET: CONNECTING THE GENERATIONS

"In every conceivable manner, the family is link to our past, bridge to our future."
Alex Haley

Traditions connect families across generations and over time. As family members from multiple generations gather to share traditions, children can learn about their cultural or religious heritage. Many family traditions revolve around specific foods, music, seasonal or cultural events, or other activities of importance to your family. Your child can learn about where he comes from and your family values as you teach him how to prepare special foods, hunt or fish, climb a mountain, milk a cow, ice-skate, or play kick the can. Arrange for multiple generations to come together when possible. Your child can learn to make Aunt Beth's scones or Grandpa's secret sauce, whether Auntie or Grandpa is still around or not.

Current research shows that sharing family history with your child helps him connect with his inner self and learn more about who he is. It helps him develop pride, confidence, self-esteem, and motivation to keep working towards the positive things in life. A tradition of telling family stories is one of the most powerful ways to help your child develop many of the resiliency skills that will prepare him to learn and grow from his own challenges. Through stories, you can help him appreciate the values you hold dear, learn wisdom from other people's mistakes, appreciate the power of forgiveness to free him from suffering, understand the satisfaction of hard work and perseverance, and so much more.

Cal's Story

I loved visiting Grandma Call and seeing the pictures she painted in my mind as I listened to her stories. In my mind's eye, I could see her father flooding the pasture every winter to make an ice-skating rink for her family and friends. I felt I was there with her family sitting on the front porch during hot summer evenings, fanning themselves and slapping mosquitoes, singing and visiting with their neighbors.

I could imagine how exciting it was when a dashing young man, destined to become my grandfather, came courting and invited her to accompany him to the popular Saltair Resort on the shores of the Great Salt Lake, a daring 40 miles from home! The resort offered an assortment of delicious thrills—a ride on the old Bamberger Railroad, a swim in the salty lake, a picnic on the shore, a terrifying ride on the rickety roller coaster—all under the spell of newly blossoming love.

And then, there we were in Wendell, Idaho, and Grandma was a farmer's wife. My mother, Lois, was born right there in the farmhouse while Grandpa talked pigs with the doctor. Grandma kept calling for help, insisting the baby was coming, but the doctor didn't believe her and said, "No, Mrs. Call, it will be a little longer." So, the menfolk talked on and on.

It was only after Grandma yelled to her husband, "Ambrose, if anything happens to this baby, I will never forgive you!" that they came in to help her. By the time they got there, my mom was nearly delivered. I don't know if Grandpa ever lived that one down.

I learned the details of how my mom's head and face got burned by hot grease, and I felt the pain and guilt Grandma carried for more than 60 years as she described the accident. I saw her anguish as she lovingly cared for her injured baby, not knowing if she would live or die, be blinded or disfigured. She was determined to provide as much care as humanly possible to help her little girl. From my grandmother's words, I gained a deeper appreciation for my mother's struggles and triumphs. The time spent sitting at Grandma's feet listening to her stories instilled gratitude in me for who I am and for my heritage.

Parenting Strategy

Tell your child stories about your family history. Tell him about the fun, happy, good things that have happened in the family and about the hard times as well. Go back to Chapter 6 on Humor and check out Cal's story about Miss Mills's Closet or Anne's story about her neighbor telling her mom, "I'll step on your toe and call you a dumb-dumb!" Look in Chapter 4 on Forgiveness and think about Ambrose stealing the apples or Anne's divorce.

Share these stories with your child, and tell him some of your own as well. Tell him how you beat your own time in the last 10K, your cousin overcame her fear of heights, and Great-grandpa discovered a goldmine. Also tell him about the time Uncle Joe lost his job, Grandma had cancer, and you dropped out of school. Talk about how your family celebrates and savors the good times, and how they struggle through the hard times and come out stronger on the other side. Talk about mistakes family members have made, and even about tough situations that are still ongoing. None of us gets to pick our family histories, but we do get to choose what we learn from them and how we move forward.

Children who know the stories of their family's triumphs and defeats develop resiliency as they come to know at an unshakeable level that good things and bad things happen to everyone and that they are part of a long line of people who can find a way to overcome whatever happens. Fortified with this history, your child will become more resilient and able to face his own rough spots with greater perspective and confidence. Your child needs to hear stories about real life and his real family. Start today. It only takes a minute to say, "Did I ever tell you about the time...?"

Add to the history. Weave your child and his experiences into the fabric of the family story. The generations are marching on, and your child is a part of the ongoing saga. Tell him stories about when he was born, what he was like as a baby, all of his funny, scary, crazy shenanigans. Tell him the stories, and then tell them again. Just as family photo albums preserve family memories, telling and retelling stories about your child and his antics, triumphs, and—very carefully and with great love and sensitivity—even his missteps and how he overcame them, creates a strong family narrative. Help him see the growth he's already had and appreciate his unique personality and strengths.

Maybe you'll decide to take it even one step further and write these stories down or help your child write them down or illustrate them. Whether or not you write them down, make it a tradition for your child to hear you say, "Remember when you
_____?"

This is personal. This is family. This is life changing.

GOOSEBERRY ICE CREAM: THE RHYTHMS OF LIFE

"Although no one can go back and make a brand new start, anyone can start from now and make a brand new ending."
Carl Bard

Some tremendously important family traditions happen only once a year or only during a certain time of year. These seasonal traditions help establish a familiar rhythm to the structure of your child's life. Repeated over the years, they become treasured events to which your child will look forward in good times and not so good times. On Christmas Eve we..., on my birthday we always..., after the first snow of the year we would..., for Halloween we....

Cal's Story

Every summer, Grandpa Call made homemade gooseberry ice cream, using his kid-powered ice-cream maker. We knew we were in for a treat when he got that twinkle in his eye and asked, "Who wants gooseberry ice cream?" We always looked forward to his playful teasing and to eating this special treat together.

Making this ice cream was quite a project and took the whole family working together. Grandpa gathered the secret ingredients and surveyed our little band, taking measure of how much each of us had grown since the last summer. Then he began assigning the task of cranking the kid-powered ice-cream maker. The little ones took their turns when the cranking had just begun and was easy. The "lucky" bigger ones took over when the ice cream was nearly done and the crank got harder and harder to turn. Excitement built with each final round of the crank until we were bursting with anticipation.

Finally, Grandpa would announce it was ready and would carefully lift the precious pail out of the salty ice slurry, wipe it clean, open the lid with a flourish, and begin scooping big spoonsful of gooseberry ice cream into our bowls. Eagerly, we waited for our first taste of the most delicious banana ice cream ever made. He couldn't fool us, because we all knew that Grandpa had substituted bananas for gooseberries, and we looked forward to it.

We loved this tradition and always had fun eating "gooseberry" ice cream, talking and laughing with each other. Grandpa and Grandma loved to have their children and grandchildren with them. We all learned the "secret" recipe for how to transform gooseberries into bananas, creating a delicious treat and a wonderful family experience.

Parenting Strategy

Traditions repeated throughout the year build a strong foundation of resiliency. Little shared moments create bonds that hold the family together. Simple rituals repeated over and over bring pleasure and happiness now as they weave ties strong enough to carry us through the trials that come to us all. The traditions you choose to carry on should reflect your personality and values. Are you a fun-loving jokester, witty, playful, serious-minded, calm, quiet, boisterous, civic-minded, outdoorsy, intellectual, musical, athletic?

If you already have family traditions you love, hold on to them, strengthen them by telling stories and reminiscing about the times you've shared, and involve younger family members in the planning and preparation. If you feel your family could benefit from some new traditions, go ahead and start one that fits you! Flag football after Thanksgiving dinner, a special pillowcase or plate for birthdays, planting an extra row in your vegetable garden for the food bank every summer, that seven-layer Jell-O salad Grandma always made on the Fourth of July, scones for Christmas morning. Most importantly of all, decide to start now. Give it a try. If it works, do it again. If not, move on until you find ones that do.

Once you find traditions that work for you, repeating them year after year will create a sense of stability and give your child cherished moments to look forward to. When your child doesn't make the team or is having trouble making new friends after the family moves, the strength of these traditions can help her have the resiliency to keep going, knowing without a doubt that there will be the same gooseberry ice cream at Grandpa's next summer, and the next, and the next.

THE POWER OF GRILLED CHEESE SANDWICHES: MEANINGFUL ROUTINES

"If you want your children to turn out well, spend twice as much time with them and half as much money."
Abigail Van Buren

Make it a priority to set aside family time in your busy schedule every week. Your family needs quality, weekly time to create the kind of ties that support your child's growing resiliency. Making weekly family traditions a routine will ensure these experiences happen consistently, which is essential for two reasons: (1) it sends a clear message to your child that he is important enough to be on your calendar, and (2) it gives you regular times to communicate your love, values, hopes, and dreams through shared experiences.

Cal's Story

As teenagers, my sisters and I had friends over almost every Sunday evening. After a while, we didn't have to invite them, because they knew our parents set that time aside for them and had an open-door policy. These gatherings were relaxing, enjoyable, and predictable. We ate, talked, played games, and maybe even watched TV once in a while. The menu was always the same: grilled cheese sandwiches and hot chocolate. No one ever complained about the food or asked for a different menu.

I guess that anyone who didn't like grilled cheese learned to like it, or maybe they just enjoyed being there so much that it didn't matter. I am aware of only one person who didn't like the sandwiches, but he learned to enjoy them (and eventually married my younger sister).

Our friends knew they were welcome, they could be themselves, and they could speak openly and honestly. They could joke with our parents or have a serious conversation. They laughed when my dad teased them and listened when he gave advice. Reminiscing about these activities makes me realize the sacrifices my parents made as they opened their home every Sunday for our friends. We were far from wealthy, but every Sunday night they provided love, friendship, and a safe haven for our friends and us.

Looking back, I realize that we really were wealthy in all the riches that mattered most. My parents were rich in patience, tolerance, friendliness and shared this wealth by welcoming all, being nonjudgmental, accepting, and loving and creating warmth within the home. As I think about these Sunday night get-togethers, I realize that my parents were teaching us these essential resiliency skills through their example. They could have tried to talk to us about these skills, but they had a better way. And now you know why, in my life, grilled cheese sandwiches truly are a power food.

Parenting Strategy

Investing the time to create regular weekly and monthly traditions will pay off with high rewards. Regular opportunities to share time, talk, play, and learn together will help your child develop a sense of your dependable commitment to him. He knows that you will be there for him no matter what happens in your lives.

In your child's life, there will be ups and downs. Maybe his best friend is moving away, his dog died, the person he likes doesn't like him, or he is being pressured for sex before he is ready. Maintaining regular weekly traditions of shared family time will give him added stability and the resiliency he needs to help him through it.

Simple, shared pleasures can become treasured memories: reading the comics out loud in bed on Sunday morning, Friday night family movie slumber parties, Taco Tuesdays, crossword puzzles on Saturday afternoons. Have fun together. Teach your child the skills he needs to join you in doing the things you like to do, whether that is dancing the jitterbug, rock climbing, or whipping up a batch of chocolate chip cookies. Let him take the lead sometimes and do things your child likes to do. You may be surprised what you can learn from him, and it is a powerful experience for a child to be in charge once in a while.

Being together on a regular basis makes it so much easier and more natural to talk, develop deeper connections, practice better communication, and demonstrate your values. Perhaps you value service; make it a tradition to serve others together. Perhaps you value gratitude; make it a tradition to express it. Perhaps you value hard work; take on a project and enjoy the satisfaction of working hard on it together.

We know that we already mentioned this, but it is so important that we want to say it one more time. Are you ready? Though it is hard, if you take on this challenge, you and your family will join the elite ranks of the extraordinary and reap the benefits week after week and year after year. You will be working towards a dream of sustained quality family time. So here it is: at least once a week, or even better, daily if possible, turn off all of your screens. Your children's screens, your screens. All of them. Start as small as you have to, and slowly build over time for this most important tradition of connection. If you haven't been doing this, start with even just five or ten minutes if that's all you can manage at first.

Start with activities you know your child loves and ones that are very engaging, such as playing a game of ball, going sledding, or drawing with chalk on the sidewalk. Gradually increase your time spent doing this until you have a tradition of quality connection time. You, your child, and your relationship will be transformed in amazing ways that will last forever. Above all, as you share experiences, your child will come to know you, and you will come to know him in a deeper, more meaningful way. He will feel treasured and important, and this will help him grow ever more resilient week by week by week. A strong sense of shared family traditions will become your child's indestructible resiliency anchor as he moves forward through life.

Chapter 8

WISDOM

"Wisdom never comes to those who believe they have nothing left to learn."
Charles de Lint

AN ALLIGATOR'S DINNER SITTING IN A CANOE: WARN AND TEACH

"The disadvantage of becoming wise is that you realize how foolish you have been."
Evan Esar

Wisdom is difficult to define, yet most people agree that they recognize it when they see it. Key attributes of wisdom include an impressive combination of the ability to think and act based on experience, knowledge, good judgment, insight, and common sense.

There are three main types of wisdom: *practical wisdom* (think of Abraham Lincoln and Benjamin Franklin), *philosophical wisdom* (think of Socrates and King Solomon), and *benevolent wisdom* (think of Martin Luther King, Jr. and Mother Teresa). There are also everyday role models of each type of wisdom. These could be a grandparent, an aunt or teacher, a favorite writer, a character in a TV show or a movie, a spiritual leader, or even a barber or the clerk at a neighborhood store.

Your child needs you to guide her in developing the wisdom she needs to make choices that help her move forward in life rather than hold her back. You need wisdom yourself to balance how much you let your child make choices for herself and how much you shelter her by making choices for her. Finding the right balance is difficult yet essential to living resiliently.

Cal's Story

Several years ago, Anne and I were in Florida spending time with our family. One of the activities we planned was an outing to the Everglades where we rented a couple of canoes so we could paddle around and observe the alligators in their natural environment. Before setting off, the park rangers gave us instructions about respecting the alligators and not getting too close. I thought their advice was wise and appreciated their instructions.

Anne, our two sons, our daughter-in-law, and three of our grandchildren went first, while I stayed behind with the younger ones. They returned in high spirits, having enjoyed a wonderful time paddling around and spotting gators. Now it was my turn. I hopped into the canoe with our oldest son and his wife, and off we paddled. By now, I guess it should be obvious that there is some excitement coming or I wouldn't be telling this story. The truth is, we tipped over the canoe with an alligator less than a hundred yards from us.

Now, the important part of this story is *how* the canoe tipped over. My son started teasing me about the alligator and, trying to be funny, he said, "If we tip over, Dad will scream like a girl!"

Playfully, I responded, "Oh yeah? Watch this!" and gently rocked the canoe. Unfortunately, my attempt to be funny quickly turned into a dangerous situation as we capsized. We tried to get the canoe righted but couldn't. We ended up doing the most natural thing when faced with mortal danger: we started laughing.

There are three possible reasons our lives were spared: (1) the mishap occurred within a few hundred feet of park rangers who rescued us posthaste, (2) the alligator needed glasses and didn't see us, or (3) it wasn't hungry.

Parenting Strategy

Obviously, the lack of wisdom and poor example from a responsible adult created a negative impression on our grandchildren. Cal says that, from this experience, he learned that we can warn and teach our children to recognize life's alligators, and we can even help them understand how to avoid these alligators. Without setting a positive example, however, our teaching may lack effectiveness. A much better plan is to let them know by word *and* deed that they can safely look to us for guidance and protection.

After you model wise decision-making, start to let your child make her own age-appropriate choices *and* live with the consequences. Start small, and use your own wisdom to protect your child from choices that are beyond her age and wisdom. A younger child can be given the freedom to choose how fast to run in the grass at the park but not whether to cross the street alone. A teen can be expected to choose for herself whether to study before or after dinner or to work out at the gym or hang out with a friend but not whether to experiment with underage drinking or reckless driving.

Use wisdom to balance letting your child paddle out on new adventures and protecting her from the alligators of life. Put some thought into why you make the rules you make and openly share your reasoning with your child. Talk about how one part of you may want one thing, like staying up late and watching TV, and another part wants something else, like going to bed early and getting a good night's sleep. Walk your child through how you make your decisions. It's never too early, or too late, to start.

To the five-year-old at the park, you might say, "Of course you want to pick the flowers. They are so pretty and fun to hold, *and* they belong to everyone in the city. Let's leave them where other people can see them, too, and we can see them again when we come back." To the teenager, you might say, "It would be lots of fun to ride to the game on the back of your friend's cool new motorcycle. I am sure it's embarrassing to have your parent say no and not let you do what the other kids are doing, *and* it's important to me to balance safety and fun. There are several steps to prepare for safety. You will need to purchase and wear a helmet and protective gear. (The motorcyclist's leathers are not just a fashion statement.) You will need to find, pay for, and complete an accredited motorcycle safety course before you can be a passenger or a driver. You can be a passenger if the driver has also completed a safety course and has at least six months of driving experience. Now, let's talk about another way for you to get to the game today." Most importantly, expect your child to own and fully experience the results of her choices, then help her consider resilient course corrections along the way.

MRS. WIGGS: LEARN FROM OTHERS

"It's not what you look at that matters, it's what you see."
Henry David Thoreau

People with great wisdom maintain a sense of optimism in the face of life's trials. They understand that life has its ups and downs and remain confident that events will play out over time and that life will work out.

Wiser people tend to:

• Make better decisions

- Have better relationships
- Find greater satisfaction in life
- Experience fewer negative emotions
- Let go more easily of depressive ruminating
- Report higher levels of well-being, especially as they age
- Live longer

Cal's Story

When I was a child, I received a book for Christmas entitled *Mrs. Wiggs of the Cabbage Patch*, by Alice Hegan Rice. Mrs. Wiggs is a poor woman, living in dilapidated housing with her four children. She is an uneducated but wise woman with a lifetime of experience she is willing to share with all who will listen. It doesn't matter to her if they are rich or poor.

Her advice is simple, homespun, down-to-earth, and spoken in her own unique way. Although her grammar is far from standard, her advice is stellar. Below are a few examples.

> "…it ain't never no use puttin' up yer umbrell' till it rains!"

> "'Tis one thing to be tempted, another thing to fall."

> "It is easy enough to be pleasant
>   When life flows along like a song,
> But the man worthwhile is the one who will smile,
>   When everything goes dead wrong."

> "'How'd they ever know it was my birthday?' exclaimed Mrs. Wiggs, in delight. 'Why, I'd even forgot it myself! We'll [take] the cake fer the party to-night. *Somehow, I never feel like good things b'long to me till I pass 'em on to somebody else.*'"

Parenting Strategy

People like Mrs. Wiggs who reflect on life experiences and are willing to share can be valuable sources of wisdom and save your child from many unnecessarily painful bumps along the way. Help your child realize that trying everything out for himself can be a painful and expensive way to learn wisdom. Much can be gained by listening to and observing others. The neighbor kid just rode his skateboard off the garage roof and broke his wrist? Maybe your child doesn't have to try it for himself.

Tell your child stories about things that happen at home, at work, in the neighborhood, on the news, or in the paper. For example, you could talk about the conflict of values between speed and safety when taking food out of the oven. You could discuss a story you heard on the news about a five-car pileup on the freeway during a bad snowstorm. Ask, "I wonder how many of the people involved really needed to be out driving right then." Talk about how important it is to stop and think about choices, to consider both the short- and long-term consequences of decisions, to weigh the possible impact of our choices on others, and to take into account multiple factors. In this little example, that would be the road conditions, posted speed limit, visibility, etc.

Encourage your child to tell you stories. Really listen, then put your heads together and identify his values and priorities. Model observing your own experiences, learning from them, and sharing what you learn. Talk about learning from others' experiences as a path to wisdom. By telling your child stories of your own life—your roadblocks and your successes—you will help him develop the wisdom to make wise choices in his own life.

The Boy Who Stole the Mouse's Cheese: Examine Experiences

"One's philosophy is not expressed in words; it is expressed in the choices we make…and the choices we make are ultimately our responsibility."
Eleanor Roosevelt

Very young children do not have the knowledge and experience to be wise in their thoughts and actions. Even as they grow older and gain some knowledge and experience, they do not necessarily become wise. You can cultivate wisdom in your child by helping her discover new ways to think about the knowledge she has. Show her how to analyze knowledge, separate it into parts, consider it in new ways, explore similarities and differences, and make new connections. A young girl is offered a taste of a new ice cream at the store: how can she use her knowledge and experience to decide whether to buy the new one or stick with her old favorite?

Help your child examine her experiences. What worked or didn't work for her? What did she learn from it? What was important and why? How could thinking about this experience change her future choices? For example, a teenage girl spent last summer hanging out with a group of friends, going swimming, hiking, and playing tennis, and this summer she has a chance to attend a computer class at the local college. She loves hanging out with her friends and relaxing, but she is also thinking about a career in computer science and this might be an opportunity for some meaningful hands-on experience. How will she choose? How will she examine and learn from her experiences? How will developing new insights impact her attitudes, values, and behaviors?

Cal's Story

Recently, Anne and I attended an event where a man from Mexico spoke. He only spoke for a few minutes, but I was intrigued by his story. When he was six years old, his mother jumped when she saw a little mouse in the kitchen. He didn't know if she jumped from surprise or fear, but he remembered that she took immediate and decisive action.

His mother went to the refrigerator, took out the cheese, and cut off a small piece. She went to the cupboard, found a mousetrap, put the cheese on it, activated it, and put it in the middle of the kitchen floor. She told her son leave it alone and to not touch it. A short time later, she left to run an errand. Before leaving, she once again warned her son not to play with the trap. However, what he heard her say was, "Take the cheese."

He liked cheese a lot, so, after his mother left, he decided to eat the cheese. He reached down to take it, but, before he could get it, the trap snapped and caught his finger. It really hurt, but all he could do was cry until someone came to help him. They got the trap off, but it still hurt.

What do mice and children have in common? Cheese! With our help, at least our children can learn to know when it is safe to eat it.

Parenting Strategy

This story is a great reminder of the importance of explaining your thinking. How often do you give your child directions or a rule to follow without taking the time to explain the reasoning behind your decisions? Sharing your thoughts about why you want your child to do something will help her develop wisdom as she begins to see the process by which you make decisions and choices. Talk to her about what you are hoping she will learn and how you think what you are asking her to do will accomplish that. By doing this, you will be preparing your child to make wise choices on her own, potentially avoiding costly pitfalls of shortsighted actions.

The power of being a role model cannot be overstated. As a parent, you are a role model whether you want to be or not. Your child does observe how you live your life and draws conclusions from what she sees. So here is a three-step proposal:

1. Think about what your child would conclude is important to you by simply watching what you do and say, how you spend your time, how you treat others, etc.
2. Take time to share with your child how you make choices. Walk her through how you decide what job to take, where to go on vacation, how much to spend on a house or a car, or how to spend your weekend.
3. Now help her apply this same process to her choices: how to pick out a toy, how to choose a friend, what to do after school, how to earn and spend money. Teaching your child to clarify her values and make choices consistent with those values will give her a foundation for wisdom in her life.

DUMB HORSE OR DUMB BOYS?: NEW PERSPECTIVES

"The pessimist complains about the wind; the optimist expects it to change; the realist adjusts the sails."
William Arthur Ward

When Cal's dad was in his 90s, he explained that his philosophy of life was to "let the water run where it runs!" He went on to say that he did not mean that he lived his life wandering hither and thither, but rather that he tried not to worry about those things he couldn't control and focused his energy on those things he could control. For example, he couldn't control what people thought of him, so he developed a standard of living he thought was best for him and lived accordingly. He recognized what he could control were his choices and attitude.

Part of being wise comes from the ability to see life from multiple perspectives and to recognize that your way of looking at the world is not the only one. Help your child step back and see the world through a wider angle lens, then apply his new perspectives in his own life. Guide him to consider how new ways of looking at life might influence his attitudes and values and therefore how he might choose to act.

Cal's Story

It was one of those hot, lazy summer afternoons with not much to do. Morning chores were done, and my two cousins and I were relaxing, biding our time until time for evening chores on Uncle Quinn's ranch. We decided to go horseback riding, but we had just one horse among the three of us, so we rode bareback. That day, I decided it was the dumbest horse I ever rode.

I don't remember whose idea it was to ride that horse, but I do know it was a lousy idea. I guess it really doesn't matter whose idea it was, because I was the one choosing to get back on after falling off several times. I had never experienced a horse like this one. Why? Well, it only had two speeds: run and stop. As soon as we hopped on, it took off running and didn't slow down until it came to a fence. When it stopped suddenly, we flew through the air until we hit the ground.

What could we do but pick ourselves up and jump back on? As soon as we were on, it took off running again and didn't stop until we came to another fence, and guess what? Same results. After landing on the ground several times, we realized we weren't going to change that horse's habits, and, besides, it was getting late and we needed to get back to the barn to do our chores.

We all knew that when we reached the barn, we would be hitting the ground again. Sure enough, that is exactly what happened, except this time the ground was harder and more unforgiving for me. I lay on the ground, holding my elbow, unable to bend it, trying to man up without crying (I can't remember if I succeeded). All I do remember is that my grandmother showed up pretty quickly and took me to the hospital. I went into surgery that evening.

Parenting Strategy

Remember the quote from Nelson Mandela in Chapter 1: "The greatest glory in living lies not in never falling, but in rising every time we fall"? Implied in this thought is that we will learn from our experience. When your child falls, literally or otherwise, help him think through his actions. Perhaps he had a great plan and can get up and try it again with a reasonable chance of success. Perhaps he failed to consider an important factor or misinterpreted the situation and should make adjustments before he rises, changes his plan, and takes a new course. It would be pure foolishness for us to keep falling, never examine why we fell, and repeat what we did without gaining wisdom in the process.

Cal and his cousins provide a beautiful illustration of such foolishness. They repeatedly did the same thing and didn't correct their course until someone got hurt. They were stuck on one idea of fun without considering other options.

Help your child learn from unwise choices when he makes them, which he will. Even better, help him learn to think through his choices before he takes action. Practice seeing things from multiple perspectives.

Go back to the story about the Blue Plate Special in Chapter 4 for more ideas on developing greater empathy, the ability to put yourself in someone else's shoes. Make it a habit to ask: What's the best possible outcome? The worst? How could this choice impact you? Someone else? Your health and safety? Someone else's health and safety? What are the short-term and long-term consequences? Can you think of a better way?

Celebrate when your child makes wise choices, big and little. Homework done before screen time? High-five! Big brother helped little sis find her favorite stuffed animal without being asked? Tell him thank you, then share the story at dinner with the whole family. Chores done early? Hooray! Let's go play a game together!

DON'T BE A "T***!": GET THE WHOLE STORY

"The only true wisdom is in knowing you know nothing."
Socrates

Part of being wise is the ability to recognize our own limitations. Wise parents are thoughtful and self-reflective, consider alternatives, and have the humility to know that they don't know it all. They use empathy to put themselves in other people's shoes and try to see the world through their eyes. When they think they understand, they ask and check it out: "Did I get that right?"

A pattern of open communication in the home, sharing experiences, thoughts, and feelings will protect you and your family from jumping to wrong conclusions and unfairly judging each other.

Cal's Story

I couldn't believe it when some stranger called me a name, which I will not use, but I will simply substitute with the letter "T." You can decipher the word by filling in the blank: "Tu_d." Why would someone call me that name, when everyone knows that I am a nice, thoughtful, sensitive grandfather who always tries to do what is right? It was a silly misunderstanding, yet I was the one who was verbally attacked and suffered irreparable psychological damage. I was labeled, chewed-up, and spit out of this stranger's mouth.

Here's what happened. My son, his family, and I were driving across the country. We were a two-car caravan in my son's "small" family car and his big 12-passenger van. We stopped at a gas station in Sidney, Nebraska. My grandson and I were in the "small" car and pulled up to the pump. His parents pulled up in the big van, but we hadn't left enough room for them to use the pump they planned on using. My exceptional daughter-in-law, Jenny, jumped out of the van and told her son to move the car to another pump so they could use ours. Her request made some sense to us because our car was more maneuverable.

Jenny and the stranger were both offended when they heard my response: "I won't move...go back to the van..." Immediately, the man with the mouth told Jenny that I was a "T," and she could use his pump because he was done. On the surface, this man had a right to think I was a pompous "T," but if he had heard the entire comment, he would have called me a Saint or an Angel instead. So, what changed me from a "T" to an "Angel"? It was the part neither he nor Jenny heard that made the difference. I said, "I won't move, but, if you go back to the van and wait a minute, you can pull up, and I will pay for your gas."

This man's strong reaction was understandable, but incorrect, because he didn't have the whole story.

Parenting Strategy

In any given situation, there is so much information available to us that we literally cannot process all of it, so our brains use shortcuts to sort out what information is important. This is essential to functioning from minute to minute, but it can lead us to misread a situation and jump to the wrong conclusion.

Help your child develop the habit of seeing the whole picture more clearly. Start with physical objects and places. If you are walking around town, point out five beautiful things and five ugly things. Talk about how the area is both lovely and unsightly. Let your child take a turn. Can she find five sounds that are pleasing and five that are obnoxious to her? Or five things that are soft to touch and five that are rough? What does this mean about the place? Is it ugly, unpleasant, and rough? Or is it beautiful, pleasing, and soft? Can it be both? Over time, extend the discussion to people. Everyone has strengths and flaws. None of us is perfect, yet it is easy to notice the imperfections in others. Make it a family habit to be aware of both.

Pay particular attention to how you speak of others in front of your child, even if you think she is not listening. Children have "very big ears" and often hear a lot more about what is going on than we think. What do you say about the homeless person on the corner, the neighbor whose house needs painting, or the friend who lost his job? Do you focus on the negative and jump to conclusions? When you see a need, do you find ways to help? Use everyday events to show your child how to see the whole person and situation and to respond with kindness and generosity: the pregnant woman struggling to pick up the bag she dropped, the elderly man pulling on a heavy door, the child lost and crying in the aisle at the grocery store. Take your child to the local homeless shelter or food bank and give service. Treat those who are struggling with respect and consideration. As you do, wisdom will flourish in your family.

When you think about it, wisdom is at the core of all resiliency. Without wisdom, we would never learn from our experiences. We would be doomed to repeat the same mistakes over and over again. Thomas Edison didn't create so many wonderful inventions because he tried the same thing ten thousand times; he learned something from each attempt and then came up with a new idea. Now *that* is wisdom.

Chapter 9

VALUES

"When your values are clear to you, making decisions becomes easier."
Roy E. Disney

A Penny's Worth of Honesty: Teach by Example

"Honesty is the best policy. If I lose mine honor, I lose myself."
William Shakespeare

Values are attitudes or standards for actions, our internal compass that guides priorities and choices. Being clear about our values empowers us with confidence in how we live and why. They help us sort through conflicting benefits and downsides and guide us to make decisions we feel good about.

Shared family values clarify expectations, help children make good choices, and strengthen family bonds. It is worthwhile to regularly review your personal and family values. Consider values that apply in various aspects of your life:

- Social values, such as being respectful or giving generously
- Political values, such as protecting the rights of all or obeying the law
- Religious or spiritual values, such as showing compassion

or giving service
- Work values, such as doing your best or saving a portion of your income
- Moral values, such as contributing to the world or taking personal responsibility
- Recreational values, such as spending time together outdoors or balancing family and individual time

You are most influential as a parent when you teach by example, are humble enough to acknowledge your own imperfections, and keep trying.

Cal's Story

In August of 1974, I waved goodbye to the University of Tennessee and pointed a U-Haul truck towards Utah, accompanied by my brand-new diploma and my son Paul, who was almost four. My wife, Carol, had recently been diagnosed with ovarian cancer and flew home. We were going to stay with my parents until I could find a job.

When we arrived at my parents' home, it didn't take long for Paul to make friends in the neighborhood. One crisp autumn afternoon while he was playing outside with them, a truck stopped in front of the neighbor's house. It was loaded with beautiful red apples. You can imagine how the boys' mouths must have watered as they longed for those apples. All the boys wished the deliverymen would invite them over and share an apple with them, but he didn't. The boys watched as a man carried a bushel of apples to the neighbor's house. The neighbors weren't home, so he left them on the front porch. The boys took this as a sign that they were invited to help themselves, and that is exactly what they did.

Paul was a thoughtful boy who knew that his mom was in the house recovering from her cancer treatment and that she loved apples, so he brought one home for her and another for Grandma. Proudly, he presented his gifts to them. He was sure they would be happy and enjoy the apples, but the first thing his mom asked was, "Paul, where did you get these?" He was truthful and explained where they came from. His mom hugged him and shed a little tear for his honesty, innocence, and kind heart. "Paul," his mother said, "I appreciate that you wanted to bring Grandma and me a treat. That was special, but you took apples that didn't belong to you. Now you need to buy some apples to pay back the neighbors."

Paul and his mother decided that he should use his own money to buy four apples and apologize to the neighbors for taking their apples. I took him to the store and helped him pick out the nicest apples. With tears in his eyes, he reached into his pocket and retrieved his money. While we were gone, Paul's mom called the neighbor and explained what had happened and our plan for repaying the debt. She asked the neighbor to not just brush it off or tell Paul that it was alright. When we got home, Paul and I walked over to the neighbor's to deliver the apples. I waited out front as Paul stood crying, apologized, and handed the apples to the neighbor.

A few days later, Grandma invited Paul to go to the grocery store with her. They were in the produce section, and, as she normally did when buying grapes, she sampled one to check its sweetness. Our little Paul watched closely as Grandma selected a nice plump grape and plopped it into her mouth. This observant young boy was curious about why it was OK for Grandma to eat a grape and not pay for it, so he asked, "Grandma, did you pay for that grape?"

"No," she replied.

"Did you steal it, Grandma?"

"No, I didn't steal it," she protested, but he was confused. After all, hadn't he done something similar and was told it was stealing? What was the difference between what he did and what his grandmother did? While in the store, he asked the same question two or three more times and got the same answer each time.

Grandma paid for the groceries, put them in the car, and was driving home when Paul asked one more time, "Grandma, did you eat that grape without paying for it?"

"Yes, Paul, I did." Then Grandma asked Paul a question: "Do you think I should go back to the store and pay for it?"

Paul said, "Yes."

Grandma replied, "So do I."

Although she was almost home, she turned the car around and returned to the store. Taking Paul by the hand, she went up to the clerk who had helped her and said, "Sir, I ate a grape without paying for it. My grandson convinced me that I should come back and pay for it." With that, she plunked down a penny on the counter and left the store with a clear conscience and a happy boy.

The clerk and the people in line looked at her a little strangely, but Paul was beaming with pride. Despite the slight embarrassment caused by returning to the store to pay for a single grape, Grandma and Paul agreed that honesty in big and little things is important and should be part of everyone's life.

Parenting Strategy

Hold a family meeting and encourage everyone to help make a list of values you believe in or want to cultivate as a family. To get everyone brainstorming, talk about your family traditions, cultural background, religious beliefs, and social beliefs, and identify any values they represent. Write down all of the ideas. Discuss the meaning of each value and what it would look like if you really lived those values at home and when you are away at school, work, or wherever you go. Select four or five values to focus on right now.

Create and display a poster about the values you have chosen. This can be as simple as a list or as creative as you like, depending on the interests and age of your child. Let him be as involved as he is willing to be. This will help him feel a sense of ownership in the process.

Review your poster often. Talk about daily events and how family values influence the choices you and your child make. Discuss the dilemmas that arise when values come into conflict. For example, you may have a family value to pursue excellence in learning and another to give service. How does your child choose what to do when he is in the middle of studying for a final exam and his friend texts him in distress about an argument in his family?

Update your poster frequently as you learn and grow together as a family and refine your priorities. Families with a defined set of values are better able to stand strong and be resilient in the face of challenges.

The Toothpick: Life's Simple Pleasures

*"If I have done anything, even a little, to help small
children enjoy honest, simple pleasures,
I have done a bit of good."*
Beatrix Potter

Values guide parents' child-rearing choices and help them determine their priorities, set family rules, and make decisions. Values need to be lived repeatedly and consistently, put into action day after day. They are acquired over an extended period of time and sink deep into how we live our lives. Becoming clear about values can help you and your child:

- Know yourselves better
- Eliminate many confusions
- Articulate desired outcomes and directions
- Choose how to spend your time and energy
- Be more responsible and accountable for your own actions
- Increase self-control
- Have more respect for yourselves and others
- Develop greater empathy for those with differing values

Cal's Story

On January 13, 2015, two of my sisters, my dad's wife, and I sat in a care center with my 92-year-old father, who was in the process of transitioning from this life into the next. We all knew that we had only a few hours left with this good man, and we wanted to enjoy the time and the sweet spirit that we had together. We shared stories, and my sister Connie told a simple anecdote that I had never heard but was so typical of Dad.

162

Connie had gone to visit Dad and his wife at the care center. They had just eaten, and Dad had some food caught between his teeth. (Yes, he still had all of his own teeth.) He wanted a toothpick, so Connie went to the nurse's station to inquire whether or not they had one. They didn't, but the aide, who was always happy and willing to help, said she knew where she could find a couple for him. She entered another patient's room and asked if she could borrow a few (although I'm sure he didn't want them returned!).

Dad and Connie appreciated this simple act of kindness. After cleaning his teeth, Dad felt much better and slipped back into a familiar old habit. He let the toothpick rest on his lower lip, moving it from side to side just as natural as we remember him always doing. He was relaxed and content being with those he loved.

As I thought about this experience, I was strongly impressed with how the little comforts of life can be such a blessing to us. The moment Dad got the toothpick, he was excited because an annoying piece of food was about to be removed and he could get back to enjoying the visit.

What a great blessing it is to understand, appreciate, and share with our children the simple things of life.

Parenting Strategy

Enjoying the simple pleasures of life is one of an infinite number of important values you might choose to make a part of your life and model for your child. It is a value that is becoming crucial with the ever-increasing number of screen-time activities, expensive toys, and pressures to buy the next greatest thing.

To model this value, take a couple of minutes to let go of your own stress. Take a deep, slow inhale, followed by an extra-long exhale, letting your shoulders drop, then blink slowly three times. (This sends a message to your brain that you are safe and can let go of worry and stress for a few minutes.) Next, think of an idea for a simple activity, and then invite your child to join you. Depending on her age and interests, you might build a fort with pillows and blankets, then lie down together inside it and tell silly stories; or maybe cook s'mores on the stove top or in the microwave and enjoy making a sticky mess while you eat them; or take a walk around the block or a hike up the canyon and find five different kinds of leaves, rocks, or insects; or drop sticks into a stream from one side of a bridge, then rush over to the other side and see whose stick comes out first. Enjoy your simple pleasure experiences!

Laugh and relax together. Remember, instilling a value in your child takes repeated experiences. Whatever values you choose, find ways to make them come alive in your day-to-day life. One trip to the stream may be pleasant but alone will not cultivate a deep value for enjoying the simple pleasures of life.

LIFE IS LIKE RIDING A BICYCLE: KEEP YOUR MOMENTUM GOING

"It's all about quality of life and finding a happy balance between work and friends and family."
Philip Green

Values develop slowly over a long process of many interactions repeated over time. Use daily experiences to teach the values you want to cultivate in your family. Experience by experience, these lived values will settle deep into your child's sense of the world and who he is in it.

The values children learn serve as a guide for how to act or not act. Younger children need clear instructions and consistent messages. They are still learning the differences between right and wrong and gaining the strength and courage to choose what is right, even when it is hard. Their choices will play out at home with the family and with their teachers and peers at school, the playground, and camp.

Older children and adolescents are often influenced by the values of their peers. It is important that they have deeply embedded personal and family values to guide them through this time.

While you can actively teach values at any age, it is easier to start earlier than later. As teens grow older, they are ready to make more of their own decisions and choices, still within the reasonable limits you set. If you try to control your older child too much, he is more likely to rebel. If you step back too far and offer too few limitations, he may conclude that you don't care about him.

Expect to have setbacks and fall short of your ideals. This is natural. Don't most of us fall off the bike at least a few times while we are learning to ride it? With bikes and life, the key is to pick yourself up, climb back onto the seat, and push off again. You learn from your experience, focus on what is ahead, watch out for the rocks in the road and the sharp turns coming up, and always keep your momentum going.

Cal's Story

In the summer of 2012, my family spent a couple of days at an inn located on a farm in rural Belgium. It was a great experience for all of us, but especially for our grandchildren who had never experienced any kind of farm life.

One evening, Anne and I decided to go for a walk by ourselves, and so hand-in-hand we walked around until we came to an old barn located on the property. Curiosity got the best of us, and we decided to go inside and take a look. It brought back many memories of my childhood experiences on my grandfather's farm in Afton, Wyoming. Tacked to a wall in the barn was a piece of paper with the following message written in English: "Life is like riding a bicycle. In order to keep your balance, you must keep moving."

This simple message resonated with me, and later I learned it was a quote by Albert Einstein. Prior to this trip, Anne had bought me a nice road bike for an early birthday present. It was a beautiful bike, lightweight with the newest gears and clip-in pedals. I was excited yet nervous about riding it on the street, because I had never clipped my feet into my pedals before. I knew I needed practice, so I found a safe place to practice clipping my new bike shoes into and out of the pedals as I slowed down and stopped over and over again. I knew that I had to learn this skill until it became second nature or risk a fall.

On my first ride, even with all my practice, I carefully came to a stop at a stoplight, but forgot all about being clipped into the pedals. I lost my balance and tipped over. Fortunately, all that was wounded was my dignity.

The sign in that old Belgian barn opened my eyes to an obvious life lesson: we really must keep moving forward if we want to improve ourselves. If not, we risk losing our momentum and balance in our struggle for personal growth and development. Helping our children find balance in their lives is a self-improvement program that can and will help them in all aspects of life, in the present as well as the future.

Life really *is* like riding a bicycle.

Parenting Strategy

What do you value? As your child watches you day to day, can he tell what you value by the way you spend your time and other resources or by the way you talk about and treat your family, your neighbors, and others in your community? A huge part of creating a strong, trusting relationship with your child is teaching him your values through your words and actions and then helping him figure out his own values and how to live consistently with them. The older your child is, the more likely it is that his friends will influence his values. No matter how old your child is, be curious about who he spends time with. Get to know his friends and what's going on at his school. Find out what his friends value and how they influence your child.

Help your child learn to stand up for his values through your example. If your own actions don't reflect your values, there is no better time than now to change that! You can also help your child clarify his own values and how to stand up for them through role-plays. Let your child suggest some common dilemmas and take turns acting out different responses. Talk through various options and how things might play out. Consider the best and worst possible outcomes. Based on your child's values, does he believe those outcomes, both positive and negative, would be worth the risk?

ON BELAY: IN WORD AND DEED

"Trust is earned when actions meet words."
Chris Butler

Teach your child to define and live by her own values through direct instruction and by example. As your child develops a strong set of personal and family values, she will have a better sense of who she is and become more confident and at ease with herself. She will be grounded and less likely to be swayed by every new trend that comes along or pressure from peers. Her authenticity will lead others to trust her and look to her for leadership. Her relationships with family, friends, teachers, coaches, and others will become stronger and more secure.

Anne's Story

My father, David C. Evans, mentored hundreds of boys during his 27-year tenure as a scoutmaster. He trained and inspired his scouts to be prepared and accountable during their scouting adventures and daily lives. Every summer, he took his scouts on a weeklong backpacking trip. One summer more than 40 years ago, my dad took a group of scouts plus my 10-year-old brother, Doug, to climb Gannett Peak in the Wind River Mountains of Wyoming. In order to summit the peak, they had to climb a glacier.

My dad carefully prepared the boys, teaching them the intricacies of climbing, especially techniques to keep them safe. They learned how to belay or make an anchor. This was done by planting their pickaxe in the ice and wrapping the rope around it in a figure eight, or by positioning themselves behind a large boulder and wrapping their rope securely around the rock. They learned that these simple actions protected both themselves and their climbing partner. Using a series of anchors, climbers provide security for each other as they take turns moving along the glacier. When one climber is ready to step out on the ice, he lets his partner know by calling, "On belay." His partner responds, "Belay on," indicating that he is in position and prepared to protect his partner. From that moment on, the climber moving out onto the ice trusts his partner with his life. If the climber should slip or fall, all will be well as long as his partner is properly secured and maintains the anchor.

After summiting the beautiful peak and while still on a particularly treacherous section high on the mountain, my brother secured our dad with a body belay from behind a large boulder. Dad called out, "On belay" to signal that he was ready to move out and put himself into Doug's hands for safekeeping.

Doug responded, "Belay on," signaling that he was set and had our dad safely in his care. All was going well as Dad began down climbing below Doug. When he was about 60 feet below the anchor point, he heard panicked cries. He turned and saw two young men, not from their group, roped together but with no anchor, plummeting out of control down an icy face alongside the rocks towards a deep and deadly crevasse below.

Knowing that Doug was prepared and could be counted on, my dad called out, "Hold on for all your life!" and swung with all of his might off of the rocks and onto the icy slope, into the path of the falling climbers. As they collided, my dad miraculously grabbed the first young man and managed to hold on as the second one swooshed past them, then yanked to a stop as the rope pulled taut. Doug heroically held the anchor as the three lives hung in his young hands.

Parenting Strategy

Help your child be prepared to face her unique challenges by teaching her how to anchor her life in values capable of providing a secure foundation. With this preparation, she will be ready to step out "on belay" as needed when moments of trial come along. This story about Anne's dad and her brother Doug illustrates the power of combining direct instruction with experience. After teaching the scouts to be prepared and accountable, Dave took them out onto the glacier and let them experience it for themselves.

You can do the same. Pick one value that is important to you. Think about how and why it became important in your life. Tell your child the story. How does having this value impact how you live your life? How well do you feel you live up to your ideal for this value? What are some of your challenges? Share some examples. Have you ever had an experience in which this value came in conflict with another value that you hold dear? How did you resolve your dilemma?

The next step is to think of challenges your child faces right now and how putting this value into practice might help her face those challenges. Talk together about the personal growth and other potential benefits of doing this. Talk about any difficulties or conflicts that might arise if she did so. Help her decide if she could benefit from living by this value. If so, help her prepare and follow up with her afterwards.

Plan additional activities to reinforce your instructions. For example, when teaching your child about the value of being trustworthy, invite her on a Trust Walk. Begin by selecting a safe environment and observing it with your child, such as your backyard or living room. Blindfold your child and let her put her hand securely through your arm. Ask her to trust you as you guide her with your arm and your words around the agreed-upon area. Switch roles and rely on your child to guide you. Move out into more challenging places, such as the park or an obstacle course you set up, depending on your child's age, maturity, and experience.

WWII German Veteran: Under Duress

"Everything can be taken from a man but one thing: the last of the human freedoms—to choose one's attitude in any given set of circumstances, to choose one's own way."
Viktor Frankl

Difficult experiences test our assumptions about life, along with our closest-held values. Under duress, we learn much about what is most important to us. Viktor Frankl, renowned neurologist, psychiatrist, and Holocaust survivor, watched as guards and prisoners struggled with their values, thoughts, and actions in the desperate realities of the concentration camps. He observed that choice and action when under threat are true tests of values.

We are tested when one closely held value comes in conflict with another. You help your child develop resiliency as you believe in his ability and worth when the challenges of life test his values and beliefs. Your support through difficult times will help your child clarify and refine his values. With more clearly defined values, he will be better able to stand strong in the face of future challenges. He will also be less likely to judge others harshly when they stumble under pressure or otherwise fall short of their ideals.

Cal's Story

Some time ago, I was visiting my oldest son and his family in Stuttgart, Germany. One of my grandsons and I decided to take a walk to a nearby park and work on some stories he was writing. Shortly after sitting down, we were joined by an older gentleman, who we learned was 92 years old. He spoke decent English, and he wanted to talk.

Before long, we forgot the writing and spent more than an hour just listening and asking questions as he shared his perspective of World War II. This was the first time I had ever viewed WWII from the eyes of a German soldier. It didn't take long for us to feel his dislike, perhaps even hatred, towards Hitler. He was a veteran of the German army, and he explained how Hitler had ruined his youth. When he should have been enjoying life with his friends and studying at the university, he was dragged off to fight a war that never should have been fought.

We learned that after conscription, he was trained to fight with *panzers* (German tanks) and consequently served in a *panzer* division. He was part of the invasion of Russia and got within 30 kilometers of Moscow before being driven back. As much as he hated the war, he was quick to point out that the Russians didn't stop the German army. They were defeated by cold and hunger.

It was -50° Fahrenheit, and the troops had nothing left to eat. We were curious how they survived. We were surprised and shocked as we listened to him calmly explain that they ate their dead soldiers. I had to ask for clarification to be certain I heard him correctly. He looked at me as though he didn't understand my reaction and then added by way of clarification, "It was -50° and the bodies were safe, so we ate them. We would not have survived otherwise."

Parenting Strategy

Play the "What if?" game with your child to explore values under pressure. Pose ethical dilemmas that pit values against each other. Adapt the situations to your child's age and maturity:

- What if your brother lies about his age to get into the movie for less?
- What if your best friend turns against you and gets other people to bully and isolate you?

- What if someone you know throws up in the bathroom every day after lunch, but says that he is OK?
- What if kids at school use the words "retard" or "gay" in insulting ways?

Make it safe to explore multiple ways of handling each situation, the best and worst that could happen with each choice, and what to do next. Help your child go beyond simplistic answers. Play it out in your minds as it might happen in a real situation. You wouldn't tell your child to ride his bike in the street without helping him think about the dangers he might run into. Neither should you send him off to kindergarten or his first high school dance without first thinking things through together.

You can't plan ahead for every possibility, but you can prepare your child by working through values dilemmas together, giving him some practice ahead of time so he will know how to think through situations as they happen. With this preparation, he will be ready to face life's challenges resiliently.

This may be hard to hear, but remember: your child is watching you and learning, whether you want him to or not. You can only effectively teach what you also practice.

Chapter 10

HOPE AND OPTIMISM

"And will you succeed?
You will, indeed!
(98 and ¾ percent guaranteed.)"
Dr. Seuss

ANNE SULLIVAN: I COULD NOT ALTER ANYTHING BUT MYSELF

"Optimism is the faith that leads to achievement.
Nothing can be done without hope and confidence."
Helen Keller

When you turn on the TV or open your email, you are likely to be bombarded with negative news: another terrorist attack, global warming, violence near and far, economic uncertainty, the list goes on. Add these to the pressures of competitive sports, intense testing, and looming college admission boards, and it's no wonder that many teens and even younger children have a growing sense of gloom and hopelessness. Their despair can be seen in destructive choices such as dropping out of school, cutting and other self-harming behaviors, suicide, unplanned pregnancy, drug use, and crime. Discouraged, disillusioned children of all ages are at a higher risk for depression and anxiety disorders. They see little hope for the future and become convinced that their lives are ruined, nothing will ever get better, and there is nothing they can do about it.

Yet, both hope and optimism can be learned. Since these two words are often used together, it's easy to think that they mean the same thing. They are related, but distinct, concepts. Hope is a belief that something that is desired will happen. People who are hopeful tend to know what they want, think of multiple ways of making their desires happen, start doing what they can, and then keep on working. Optimism is a generalized sense of confidence that things will turn out well. Renowned psychologist Martin Seligman, author of the book *The Optimistic Child*, has spent years researching how optimism is learned. He observes that optimists and pessimists (those who generally believe that things will not turn out well) have distinctive patterns of thinking, and both patterns can be learned.

When something *good* happens, optimists tend to think it is:

- *Permanent* – likely to continue or reoccur. For example: "I'm a hard worker and that always pays off."
- *Pervasive* – not limited to a single situation and will happen in many different circumstances. For example: "I learned my multiplication tables; I can do the same with the state capitals."
- *Personal* – caused by something they did. For example: "I got an A on the test because I studied and was really prepared."

Pessimists tend to think it is:

- *Temporary* – short-lived and probably won't happen again. For example: "I was just lucky today."
- *Specific* – will only happen in this situation. For example: "I learned my multiplication tables, but I'm not good at geography and won't be able to remember the state capitals."

- *Impersonal* – not caused by something they did but due to other people or circumstances. For example: "I got an A on the test, but it was really easy."

When something *bad* happens, their thought patterns are just the opposite.

Optimists tend to think it is:

- *Temporary* – short-lived and probably won't happen again. For example: "My friend is upset with me, but I'm sure we can work it out."
- *Specific* – will only happen in this situation. For example: "My new boss doesn't seem to like me, but usually I can win people over."
- *Impersonal* – not caused by something they did but due to other people or circumstances. For example: "My sister doesn't want to play with me, but she's probably just tired right now."

Pessimists tend to think it is:

- *Permanent* – likely to continue or reoccur. For example: "My friend is upset with me; this always happens to me. We'll never be able to work it out."
- *Pervasive* – not limited to a single situation and will happen in many different circumstances. For example: "My new boss doesn't like me; no one ever likes me and I'll never get a good job or get ahead in life."
- *Personal* – caused by something they did. For example: "My sister doesn't want to play with me; she just doesn't like me and never will."

Notice the patterns of hope and optimism in the following story about the life of Anne Sullivan, famous for being Helen Keller's teacher and a tremendously resilient individual in her own right.

179

In 1866, Anne Sullivan was born in Feeding Hills, Massachusetts to illiterate and impoverished Irish immigrants. At the age of five, she contracted a bacterial eye disease known as trachoma, which severely damaged her sight. When she was eight, her mother died; when she was ten, her father abandoned her and her siblings. She and her younger brother were sent to an overcrowded almshouse in Tewksbury, Massachusetts. A few months later, her little brother died.

From a young age, Anne had a strong-willed personality and a determination to improve her lot in life. Another blind student residing in the same almshouse told her that there were schools for the blind where she could learn to read and write. She had a strong desire to attend one of these schools and set about trying to make that happen. She begged and pleaded until finally the administrators of the orphanage succumbed and allowed her to go to the special school.

She entered the Perkins School for the Blind as an elementary school student in 1880 at the age of 14. Right from the start, she had so many strikes against her. She had never been to school, couldn't read or write, and felt humiliated by her own ignorance. She lacked social graces, was quick-tempered, and challenged the school rules. Yet, she was also very bright and determined and advanced quickly in academics. Fortunately, a few of her teachers recognized her ability, accepted her for who she was, and encouraged her to use her talents to reach her potential.

In 1886, at the age of 20, Anne Sullivan graduated valedictorian of her class. At the graduation exercises, she shared the following advice with her fellow graduates: "Duty bids us go forth into active life. Let us go cheerfully, hopefully, and earnestly and set ourselves to find our especial part. When we have found it, willingly and faithfully perform it." In March of 1887, the school's director, Michael Anagnos, recommended Anne to the parents of Helen Keller. From that point on, Anne helped Helen turn her life around, becoming her teacher, mentor, and lifetime friend.

Many people do not realize how many challenges of her own Anne had to overcome in order to help her famous friend succeed. Later in life, Anne said this about why she was successful:

> I know that gradually I began to accept things as they were, and rebel less and less. The realization came to me that I could not alter anything but myself. I must accept the conventional order of society if I were to succeed in anything. I must bend to the inevitable, and govern my life by experience, not by might-have-beens.

All children and their families face challenges. Anne Sullivan and her famous student Helen Keller faced theirs and set an example by refusing to let self-pity, discouragement, or other adversities stop them from reaching their potential and enjoying their lives.

These two remarkable women knew that while there were many things in their lives that they could not control, they could control their response to them. This is the attitude of hope and optimism that we can help our children develop through example and encouragement. Developing an outlook of hope and optimism is a resiliency skill that will help them become stronger as they *fight* to become the kind of people they want to become.

Parenting Strategy

Notice your own patterns of thought when good and bad things happen. Do you tend towards optimism or pessimism? Now observe your child. What patterns do you see?

Whatever your child's current patterns, help her develop a stronger sense of optimism and hope with these three simple steps:

1. Maintain a calm composure when problems arise in her life or yours. Don't fall apart or catastrophize. It doesn't help to gasp and say, "Oh no, that's horrible! You are never going to have any friends now, or make the team, or get that scholarship..." Instead, exude confidence that no matter how bad things look right now, they will likely work out fine in the long run.

2. Respond with empathy when she expresses negative emotions. Listen to her story all the way through without interrupting or telling her she shouldn't feel a particular way. (This can be hard, but it is important that you do not interrupt.) Show her that you understand and let her know that you will always love her and be there for her, no matter what.

3. Without disparaging her concerns, help her to be more flexible in her thinking by seeing both the challenges and the positive possibilities ahead. Help her recall happy endings to other difficult situations. Challenge any "I'm doomed forever" patterns of thinking.

LIVING LIFE WITH DIGNITY: REALISTIC OPTIMISM

"Choose to be optimistic, it feels better."
Dalai Lama

In his research, Martin Seligman explores the value of what he calls "realistic optimism." Healthy optimism is not blind cheerfulness while ignoring obvious trouble. Realistic optimists recognize the problems and difficulties they face, work to change whatever can be changed, and move forward with hope and confidence. As Seligman teaches, the pilot of a severely disabled aircraft realistically should be worried *and* optimistically work on whatever problems might be able to be fixed.

Cultivating realistic optimism will help your child thrive in the face of life's challenges.

Cal's Story

When I first met Teddy, he was about 13 years old and lived in the house behind me. My first wife, Carol, and I were new to the community, a small coal-mining town in southeast Utah. I had just graduated with a master's degree in public health and had started my first professional job at the local health department.

The more I interacted with Teddy, the more I realized the extent of his challenges. Teddy had delays in his physical development, difficulty learning to speak, and other learning problems. His doctors and other healthcare professionals expected him to do poorly in school and be limited in sports or other physical activities, but Teddy had a secret weapon. He had a mother who was patient with him and worked hard to help him develop the qualities he needed to be successful in life. Through her loving and realistic optimism, she motivated him to unexpected heights. By the time I met Teddy, he was playing basketball with friends and boys on his church team. He played well enough to have fun, even though he would never be good enough to be on the school team. He was an average student, doing average work in school, but that was far better than his doctors ever expected.

Teddy and I had some great times together. One day, he came over to my house to show me his birthday present, a skateboard. He invited me to give it a try, and, not wanting to let him know

I was a wimp, I agreed. I lived on a hill, and he asked me to wait before I started down the hill. It seems he wanted to run to the bottom so that he could catch his skateboard when I fell off. When Teddy reached the bottom of the hill, he gave the signal and I hopped on. My life was flashing in front of me. I realized, for my wife's sake, I should jump off, which I did, and the skateboard went to the bottom without me. Teddy laughed, picked it up, waved goodbye, and went home.

We shot hoops together, laughed long and often, and talked about life and life's frustrations. Many times, he volunteered to help me with boring tasks of my job, such as making and passing out flyers, running errands, putting together information packets, etc. I learned to love and appreciate Teddy and his friendship.

One morning at about 7:30 a.m., two young neighbor girls knocked on our front door and asked for me. When I came out to greet them, they informed me that Teddy had died unexpectedly during the night. He was 15.

Naturally, I was shocked and greatly saddened when I heard of my young friend's passing. Knowing Teddy, I believe he died with dignity. Why? Because he lived with dignity. He accepted his challenges and moved forward with his life. He took advantage of his talents and used them to become the best he could be. He refused to feel sorry for himself, and he didn't try to be someone other than himself. He was not wealthy or accomplished or known outside his small community, but he lived his life with dignity.

Teddy had hopes for his future, and he had been optimistic that he could accomplish whatever he wanted to do. While he did not have the chance to fulfill all of his hopes and dreams, he accomplished much more in his short lifetime than many expected. His positivity and optimism live on in my life and in the lives of his family members. He is one of my all-time heroes.

Parenting Strategy

One of the best things you can do for your child is to help him develop hope and teach him that, while we cannot control everything in our lives, we can be realistically optimistic about our future. One way to do this is to help him accept himself for who he is and motivate him to strive to become the best he can become.

To help your child develop this kind of realistic optimism, ask him to choose one of these six aspects of life to focus on: physical appearance, social relationships, academic performance, personal health and well-being, care of physical space and belongings, or spirituality. You can repeat the exercise with the other areas later or add ones that fit your child's interests.

Next, ask your child to list everything he can think of about himself in the selected area on a piece of paper. Keep this simpler and shorter if your child is younger, more thorough if he is older. For example, if your 12-year-old child picked personal appearance, his list might look like this:

Fat, short, freckles, red hair, big nose, big hands, crooked teeth, brown eyes, clumsy.

Ask him to mark each attribute by whether he considers it to be positive (+) or negative (-).

Fat -, short -, freckles -, red hair -, big nose -, big hands +, crooked teeth -, brown eyes +, clumsy -

Many kids list more negatives than positives in the beginning, so don't worry. Go through each attribute and ask your child to replace any harsh or judgmental words with accurate descriptions. For example, the word fat carries a lot of negative connotations for many people, so replace it with a specific statement such as, "I weigh 115 pounds and would prefer to weigh 95."

Take a fresh sheet of paper and make two columns, one for positives and one for negatives. Move your child's list into the columns and start to expand his ideas. Ask him to think of any compliments he has ever received about the area you are focusing on and add those. Get a mirror and help him look at his body in a new light, noticing, for example, that while he may have freckles, he has very clear skin with few blemishes. He may get teased for having red hair, but it is thick and has a nice wave, and he has big hands and feet, much like his grandfather, who grew 10 inches in high school. Help him identify and add counterexamples to any negatives in his list. He may think of himself as clumsy because he trips over his feet while playing basketball, but his fine motor skills are great and help him excel at painting and playing the flute. Be accepting of his list of negatives and balance them with at least as many positives.

Next, ask your child to mark which things on his lists might be changeable and which are not. For example, he may be able to change his weight within the parameters set by his genetics. He could get braces to straighten his teeth, but he cannot realistically change his freckles. For qualities that cannot be changed, work with your child on learning to accept and value himself as he is. For those that can be changed, you can get more ideas by reading Chapter 11 on Dreams and Goals and reviewing the section on goal setting in Chapter 2 and the Setting Successful Goals worksheet in the appendix.

COURAGE TO TRY: THE GRIT TO KEEP GOING

"Just when the caterpillar thought the world was over,
it became a butterfly."
Proverb

Hope and optimism require courage and grit: the courage to try and the grit to keep going when things get tough. Just looking at the world through rose-colored glasses and hoping for the best is not enough. Help your child develop realistic hope and optimism by teaching her to respond to challenges with effective problem-solving skills. Encourage her to come up with her own solutions rather than always turning to you or others to fix things for her, solve her problems, or overcome her challenges. Communicate your confidence in her and, of course, lead the way by your own example.

Cal's Story

When I was a child, my mother told me the story of a young boy named Glenn who became one of my heroes. When Glenn was seven years old, he and his thirteen-year-old brother, Floyd, were responsible for getting to their one-room schoolhouse extra early each morning and lighting the fire in the old potbelly stove. The fire warmed the room, making it comfortable for the other students when they arrived.

One cold winter day, there were two problems with the potbelly stove that changed Glenn's life forever. First, there were still some hot coals glowing in the bottom of the stove from a meeting at the school the night before, and second, the man responsible for delivering the kerosene to the schoolhouse mistakenly left gasoline instead. When the brothers arrived at the school, Floyd unwittingly poured the gasoline into the stove. The gas hit the hot coals, causing an explosion, and the schoolhouse burst into flames. Both Floyd and Glenn were badly injured. With the help of another brother and a sister who were playing outside and were not burned, Floyd and Glenn walked the two miles back to their home.

Nine days later, Floyd died of his extensive injuries. Glenn suffered severe burns to both of his legs. He lost all of the flesh on his knees and shins, as well as the flesh of all his toes on his left foot. The transverse arch of his left foot, a critical structure for walking that runs from one side of the foot to the other side, was also seriously damaged. The doctor told Glenn's parents that he would never walk again and suggested amputating both of his legs. Martha, Glenn's mother, was a strong-willed woman and would not allow the surgery. The doctor pled with her, as he explained that it was best for Glenn and would aid in his recovery, but Martha stood firm, and the doctors backed down.

In his book, *Never Quit*, Glenn describes some of his struggles and painstaking progress.

> Slowly, I pushed my pain-wracked body upright in bed. Bracing myself, I moved my right leg one inch toward the edge of the bed...then another inch...then the left limb the same way. Finally I got both badly burned legs over the edge and onto the floor....Sweat broke out on my body. My head was reeling. Then I reached for the sturdy armchair by my bed. By grasping its arms I slowly pulled myself upright on the floor. Weakly I fell onto the chair seat. I rested for a moment, my breath coming in gasps. Using one arm of the chair as a crutch, once again I pulled

myself to my feet and began to inch my way around the chair. Then I collapsed again…how my legs hurt![1]

Glenn's injuries were so severe that they could easily have stopped him, but they didn't. He had hope, and he believed in himself. He was optimistic that he would walk again. He knew it would be difficult and that he would have to work hard and even suffer serious pain. He developed his own personal and very unconventional training program. He hung onto the tail of the family horse or a milk cow and learned first to walk and eventually to run as the animals pulled him around the barnyard.

Glenn Cunningham, the determined young boy full of hope and optimism, went on to become the premier miler of his day, winning the Kansas State High School championship, the national high school championship, two NCAA titles, and ten AAU national titles. He also ran in two Olympics and reached many other milestones in his life. In 1932, he was awarded the James E. Sullivan Award for America"s greatest amateur athlete. All of his success started with the belief that he could do it, the optimism that he wouldn't be stopped, the work ethic to train, and the courage to try. Later in his life he said, "As long as you believe you can do things, they're not impossible. You place limits on yourself mentally, not physically."[2]

Parenting Strategy

Your child will gain confidence and hope and will feel more optimistic about her future when she learns to solve her own problems as they arise. Teach her effective problem-solving skills using the following steps:

---

1 Tanner, B. "Cunningham's Character Made Him a Champion." *The Wichita Eagle*, April 5, 2004.
2 Ibid.

1. **Pinpoint the precise source of problems.** Avoid jumping to conclusions. If your child is suddenly having a hard time sleeping, explore what's going on in her life. What's different now than before?

2. **Encourage her to express her emotions.** See the world through her eyes and accept her feelings and thoughts about her life. Is she worried about something? Feeling sad, hurt, or angry? Maybe she is excited about a project at school or her friend's upcoming birthday party.

3. **Brainstorm multiple solutions.** Write them all down, even ones that seem crazy at the time. This will help the creative juices start flowing, and your child will likely come up with great ideas that you would never think of. Would you think of hanging onto a horse's tail to learn how to walk again?

4. **Evaluate all of the solutions.** Talk about the pros and cons. Eliminate any that you feel are unsafe or unwise.

5. **Let your child choose the solution she likes best.** This is her life after all!

6. **Help her set up a timetable.** Agree on a timeline for implementing her choice and checking back in with her on her progress, and then let the experiment begin.

7. **Review her progress together.** At an agreed-upon time, celebrate her efforts and then go through these steps again to create adjustments if she is not getting the results she would like.

MY BOYHOOD DREAM: BASEBALL HEROES

"Talent is cheaper than table salt. What separates the talented individual from the successful one is a lot of hard work."
Stephen King

Hope and optimism have a strong interconnection with hard work and perseverance. Having hope and an optimistic belief that effort will pay off motivates us to keep working; working hard and staying on task leads to accomplishments that help us have hope and optimism about the future. Developing a pattern of hard work is so vital to resiliency that we devoted Chapter 13 to it. As you read this chapter on hope and optimism and the chapter on hard work, you will begin to see more clearly how they connect together.

There is a legend about a Scottish king, Robert the Bruce, who led his army to battle against the British over and over again, only to be defeated each time. Exhausted and discouraged, King Robert went into hiding. During a terrific storm, he took refuge in a cave where he watched a tiny spider trying to cast its web across the roof of the cave. Repeatedly, the web failed to catch, and the spider patiently started over again. Finally, on the seventh try, success! It is said that Robert took hope from watching the spider's persistence. He left the cave, regrouped his army, fought hard, and defeated the British in the next battle.

This little tale has survived because of the principles it illustrates. In order to succeed, we need to find a reason to have hope and optimism about the future and a willingness to work to make our dreams come true.

Cal's Story

When I was a young boy, it was my dream to play baseball. My boyhood heroes were Mickey Mantle, Yogi Berra, and Whitey Ford. I loved watching Saturday baseball games and listening to the legendary broadcaster, the colorful Dizzy Dean who was well known for butchering the English language. As an example, when a teacher criticized his use of the word "ain't," he responded on air, "A lot of folks who ain't sayin' ain't, ain't eatin'. So, Teach, you learn 'em English, and I'll learn 'em baseball."

In the summer, my friends and I played baseball nearly every day, sometimes twice a day. We loved the competition and camaraderie of playing the game we loved. Oh, yeah, sometimes we would argue, yell, and even push each other a bit in the heat of the moment, but we remained friends, finished the game, walked home together, and left any disagreements on the field. To this day, I remember and laugh at the insults my friend Bill gave his younger brother. Bill would say something like, "Jim, if you converted your brains to gasoline you wouldn't have enough gas to drive a pissant's car across a pinhead." Jim would yell something back, everyone would laugh, and it would be over.

I remember the summer I was old enough to try out for Little League Baseball. This was a big deal for me. The night before the tryout, I had a hard time sleeping as I anticipated the excitement of playing on an organized team. When morning finally arrived, I jumped out of bed, got dressed, rushed through breakfast, forgot to brush my teeth, and ran out the door to meet my friend and hurry over to the tryout.

We were the first ones there, but by the time the coaches arrived, there were a lot of other boys waiting to try out. When my time finally came, the coach put me on third base and hit ground balls to me. I fielded them and threw the ball to first base, but there was one problem: my balls only made it three-quarters of the way to the first baseman. The coach hit several more balls to me, and the results were the same. They landed between the pitcher and the first baseman. After a few minutes fielding grounders, the coach told me to line up for batting practice.

When it was my turn to bat, I was excited. I really wanted to impress the coach with my batting ability, and I did. The first pitch was a fastball, and I swung at it about the time it hit the catcher's mitt. The second throw was also a fastball, same result.

And so it was with each of the pitches thrown to me; I hit nothing but air. When the tryouts ended, my friend and I walked home together. As bad as I was, I was still optimistic about making the team. After all, it was my dream, and I believed in my ability. I was confident that I was better than I had demonstrated.

I waited all afternoon by the phone. Whenever it rang, I pounced on it, expecting a call from one of the coaches, but it never came. I was surprised and disappointed. My friend got a call, and I was happy for him.

As I think back, I realize that I was very optimistic and had hopes of making the team. I also realize that while hope and optimism are good qualities and important to success, they are not enough. What stopped me from making that team was not necessarily my lack of talent but my work ethic. Without the hard work and sacrifice necessary to become the kind of player I wanted to be, I would never reach my goal in baseball. I'll never know if I would have made the team if I had worked harder, but I know for sure that without it, I did not.

Today, I still can't hit a fastball, but the lesson I learned that day about hope, hard work, and optimism has served me well in reaching other life dreams.

Parenting Strategy

Many parents unwittingly undermine their children's sense of hope, their optimism, and their willingness to work hard by being critical. Use positive reframing instead to motivate and inspire your child. A positive reframe takes what might be considered to be a negative and finds a positive quality in it. For example, if a child is having trouble getting off to school on time, a critical parent might say, "What's the matter with you? You're always so slow. Stop dawdling; get up and get going!" Using positive reframe, this might change to, "You pay close attention to detail and like to take your time doing things. This can be a real strength and create some challenges as well, which I'm sure you can overcome. I've noticed that when you lay out your clothes and pack your backpack before you go to bed, you get off to school on time. What have you noticed?"

Here are some other examples of positive reframes:

- Quiet → thoughtful
- Noisy → enthusiastic
- Stubborn → persistent
- Silly → good sense of humor
- Rigid → organized
- Impulsive → creative

Make a game with your child of finding the positives in negative or disappointing situations. Depending on your child's age and interests, try reframing situations such as: he has to stay home from the field trip to the zoo because he has a fever; he tried out for concert choir and didn't get in; his best friend is moving away; he had a low score on the SAT. Using positive reframes in your parenting will help your child become more optimistic and hopeful about his abilities and options and more willing to work to reach his potential.

LIVE TO LIVE: THE JED NIELD STORY

"We must accept finite disappointment, but never lose infinite hope."
Martin Luther King, Jr.

People who cultivate hope and optimism enjoy a long list of benefits. They tend to adapt better and feel less distress when confronted with problems. They reframe situations to see them in the best possible light, start making plans, and get to work solving problems as they come up. They are more likely to accept things they cannot change and learn to live with them graciously. They are also more likely to notice warning signs of danger and take quick action to protect themselves and others. They are more productive and less likely to give up.

Cal's Story

My cousin Jed Nield is a man who has earned my respect. He has four children, manages a thirteen thousand-acre ranch in Idaho, and competes in rodeos as a team roper. Why is Jed so impressive to me? After all, he is not the only person with these attributes, and, in fact, there are probably hundreds of cowboys in this country who fit this description. But, in my opinion, he stands out from them all.

On January 29, 2007, Jed was working alone in a remote area of a phosphate mine doing some drilling and blasting. On this particular day, he suffered an industrial accident that changed his life forever. The huge drill he was using developed a problem, and he decided to fix it without turning it off. Unfortunately, as he leaned in to work on the drill, it caught his clothing. Immediately, he was pulled into the drill, which spun him around at 114 RPM. Finally, his clothing ripped, and he was thrown free.

This accident cost him his arm and eventually his leg. He had the presence of mind to use his cell phone to call for help (which miraculously worked in an area where it usually does not). The doctors attribute his life being saved to this call along with the extreme cold, which caused the bleeding to slow down. From this accident, Jed developed a personal philosophy for life, a philosophy that could benefit us all. Jed has chosen to live his post-accident life "living to live, not living to die." He has not let the loss of an arm and a leg, countless surgeries, and considerable pain stop him.

Even though he only has one arm and one leg, he doesn't consider himself disabled. He figured out how to rig up adaptations for his saddle and lasso and still competes as a calf roper. His only concession was to take on a partner and rope as a team instead of competing by himself as he had done before. He keeps a positive attitude and is more grateful than ever for being alive and able to work and being a husband, father, and grandfather.

Parenting Strategy

Help your child embrace his challenges and grow stronger as he faces them. Jed held on to his optimism that things will work out and used his courage and ingenuity to find ways to adapt. His injury isn't what he had planned on or hoped for, but he is able to accept what happened and move forward with gratitude for life. When your child brings up something he is struggling with, or even wishes would go away, acknowledge his hopes and desires. There is nothing wrong with having them. The problem comes when we focus too much on what we think is wrong and not enough on gratitude for what we have that is good.

Help your child balance his focus by spending at least as much energy on being truly mindful of and grateful for what he has as he spends wishing for things that can't be changed. Sometimes it can help to walk outside together, look up at the sky, and focus for one full minute on being grateful for being alive and part of this beautiful world and for having a chance today to "live to live."

Share stories about people who exemplify hope and optimism. Once you start looking, you will find them in abundance. You can start with famous people like Anne Sullivan and Helen Keller, figures from history like Robert the Bruce, athletes like Glenn Cunningham, ordinary heroes in your community like Teddy, or even your own family like Jed.

As you share these stories, notice patterns in how they think about life. Help your child come up with three strategies he can use in difficult times. Some examples of hopeful and optimistic patterns of thinking are:

- Stay calm in a crisis
- Study the situation—don't jump to conclusions.
- Something good can come out of every situation.
- Take a break if you get upset and re-evaluate when you've settled down.
- Check in with yourself on your self-care: am I tired, hungry, or distressed about something else?
- Set yourself up for success. Start small and build from there.
- Have good boundaries and say "No" when asked to do too much.

Building a strong foundation of hope and optimism sets the stage for dreaming big. As Winston Churchill said, "A pessimist sees the difficulty in every opportunity, but an optimist sees the opportunity in every difficulty." Arm your child with hope and optimism, and he will be prepared to face the world with great resiliency.

Chapter 11

DREAMS AND GOALS

"Consult not your fears but your hopes and your dreams. Think not about your frustrations, but about your unfulfilled potential. Concern yourself not with what you tried and failed in, but with what it is still possible for you to do."
Pope John XXIII

FINDING MIDDLE C: MEANINGFUL DREAMS

"If you don't know where you are going, you'll end up someplace else."
Yogi Berra

Without dreams, something inside of a child dies; life becomes a dreary slog to nowhere. Dreams begin with the thought, "What if?" They are about possibilities and can be anything from a fleeting fantasy that brings pleasure for a moment to a burning desire that gives focus to a lifetime.

Goals, on the other hand, are action steps. Ideally, parents help their children set and achieve goals that take them towards meaningful dreams. Consider the difference between two young men. One sets a goal to get a college degree, only to graduate and think, "Well, that was a lot of work, now what?" The other has a dream: maybe he dreams of helping children learn, designing buildings, or relieving pain and suffering in animals. He sets a goal to graduate from college as a step towards his dream to be a teacher, an architect, or a veterinarian. He is so much more likely than the first to move forward after completing his goal, filled with excitement and energy to take the next steps towards his dream.

The most powerful dreams align with our values. Your child may dream of a fancy new bike or the latest toy. He may see a play, attend a sporting event, or read a book with the dream of becoming an actor or musician, an NFL quarterback, or a deep-sea explorer. On reflection, he may or may not decide that pursuing a particular dream is really important to him.

Your child figuring out what he values enough to pursue is part of a wonderful process. You play an important role in helping him through that process, guiding him as he explores his dreams and decides which ones he values enough to do the work required to make them become realities.

Cal's Story

When we moved from Afton, Wyoming to Salt Lake City, Utah, my parents rented a small house. It was a little bigger than the one we left because it had an indoor bathroom. It also had a kitchen, dining room, front room, and one bedroom.

There were five of us living in this house. My two sisters and I slept in the bedroom, while my parents slept in the dining room. We had an upright piano that was placed in the arch of the dining room to give them a modicum of privacy.

When I was approximately eight years old, I had this crazy idea about my musical talent and convinced Mom to let me take piano lessons. (It is important to know that they had no extra money and doing this for me was a sacrifice for them.) They found and hired a piano teacher who was willing to come to the house to give me lessons. This man was a kind man who was patient with me (which was a requirement). He was also blind and, to compensate for his lack of vision, he had a very sensitive ear and was able to give me the help I needed.

I remember three obstacles to my learning to play the piano: (1) I didn't understand anything he said, even when I sat on the bench next to him and listened very carefully, (2) I hated to practice, and (3) I was musically flawed. Nothing made any sense, and it didn't matter whether I practiced or didn't practice—the results were the same.

Meanwhile, every week my younger sister would sit on the couch and listen to my teacher from 10 feet away. Then, after he left, she would get up and go practice what he had tried to teach me. This was a very fortunate thing for me, because it provided me a way out of this mess. All I had to do was to convince Mom to let me quit piano lessons so I could play baseball with my friends and have my sister study piano. One of the wisest decisions my Mom ever made was to let me quit and have my sister take the lessons. She became a very accomplished pianist.

As parents, it's important for us to recognize and accept the fact that our children have their own strengths, weaknesses, and unique talents. With this awareness, we can provide them with better guidance and help them grow stronger as they face their challenges.

Today, I still don't know middle C from the foot pedal, and the fact is I am OK with that!

Parenting Strategy

Encourage your child to dream big, let his imagination run free, and see his own potential. Help him stretch his vision of himself and his life, carefully balanced with guidance to keep him within the possible. Maybe your child is a senior in high school and just discovered he loves snowboarding. He is so excited and motivated to practice, willing to work hard at this new passion. Help him explore his dream and think about what he is willing to do to pursue it. Does he dream of being a professional or of riding for fun and personal pleasure?

Help him consider his values and the effort and focus he would need to pursue his dream. What would he be willing to give up in order to make this dream become a reality? Help him anticipate and overcome potential obstacles, but keep it believable. Support your child in his dreams, big and little, but wisely guide him away from truly unobtainable dreams, like qualifying for the Olympics his first season as a snowboarder.

Above all, help your child decide which dreams are just fun fantasies and which are valuable enough to set goals to make happen. Without this winnowing step, your child is at risk of setting and starting to work on goals towards dreams that aren't really that important to him, getting discouraged, and then giving up because his goals are not in support of something truly of value to him.

Help your child think about what is important to him, and share your own values. Do you value having fun as a family, or kindness, or adventure? Why is it important to you? What does it represent to you? How has it helped you or others?

Start where your child is right now. Maybe he really wants to build a Lego spaceship, make the soccer team, or have more friends. Select one meaningful value or dream, and then set one small goal that will help him move in that direction.

Start with fun goals. Do you and your child both value quality time as a family? Set goals that free up time and energy to bake cookies, take hikes, read out loud together, go on a bike ride, or whatever leads you in the direction of the things you value. Having success with pleasant goals starts a pattern that will support your child when he works on more difficult and challenging goals.

Now would be an excellent time to review Setting Successful Goals as outlined in Chapter 2.

What Is the Value of an Eagle?: The Sweet Taste of Accomplishment

"A desire presupposes the possibility of action to achieve it; action presupposes a goal that is worth achieving."
Ayn Rand

Dreams give purpose and meaning to children's lives. They inspire them to be brave and strong, to step out of their comfort zone and risk trying new things. The shy girl finds the courage to stand on stage to share her poem at the talent show or act in the school play. The football star lies down in a yoga studio seeking greater focus and flexibility.

When children have meaningful dreams, they are more accountable and make wiser choices about their use of time and energy. They begin to realize what is important to them and what needs their attention, and they become better able to let go of minor irritations and inconveniences of life that could distract and derail them.

Pursuing dreams teaches children how to stay focused and keep trying. As they experience the inevitable diversions and obstacles, they can learn how to stick with a dream they cherish. They can practice finding ways to overcome whatever challenges come their way. They can even learn how to let go of dreams when their experiences lead to changing values and priorities. Letting go of one dream can be a vital step to new, more satisfying dreams. A child may need to let go of her dream to play pro ball to pursue a new dream of being a sports medicine doctor, or let go of a dream to be a gymnast to pursue painting. You play a vital role in this process as you guide your child to really see herself living her dreams.

Cal's Story

Several years ago, I was actively involved as a youth leader with the Boy Scouts of America. I have a vivid memory of a conversation I had with a teenage boy Richard about the value to him of finishing the requirements for his Eagle Scout Award. I believed that scouting has a tremendous effect in the life of a young man and, with him being so close to earning this award, he would someday regret giving up. He was approaching his 18th birthday, and if he worked hard there was just enough time for him to earn it, if it was important to him.

During the discussion I had with Richard that evening, he asked a question I had heard many times before: "What will earning an Eagle do for me?"

I was confident in my response. "You can put it on your resume when applying for a job or on your college application, or it can help you if you join the military, etc., etc." Because this was the standard answer that adults had been using for years to motivate their charges, I was confident that it would work on Richard. He was not impressed.

"I have heard all this before," he said, "but I am involved in other activities that will help me with all those things. So, please help me understand, why do I want to become an Eagle?"

This young man had me. I was trying to apply my belief system to his life. After all, he was an above-average student, full of confidence, an athlete, a student leader, and knew what he wanted to pursue.

At this point, I had an epiphany. I had not been like this young man in the slightest way. I had not been a good student, hadn't had much self-confidence, hadn't been an athlete, being a student leader had never been on my radar screen, and I wasn't sure I had the capability to reach my goals. I could not answer him.

Over the next several days, I pondered this question. It bothered me. I really questioned the value earning this award had for me.

After much thought and earnest searching, I realized that there was a personal value in earning my Eagle Scout Award. Setting my goal for this accomplishment and working hard to reach it was the first time in my life that I had set a long-term personal goal and finished it. That was the first time I really experienced the sweet taste of accomplishment and knew that it was worth all the effort!

After thinking about this young man's question, I realized that, while earning this award was a positive benefit for me, it wouldn't necessarily benefit him in the same way. I was better able to understand and support Richard's decision to not pursue the award. I knew he was already taking steps towards his own goals and would be successful in his life.

Parenting Strategy

When our children understand the value of setting goals and putting forth the effort to reach *their* goals, they also learn resiliency. Many parents make the mistake of wanting their child to set goals to accomplish things that the parents want, not goals that are actually meaningful to their child. This is a real loss, because setting and working towards personal goals is such a great way to help a child feel and be more capable and confident. Encourage your child to decide what she wants to accomplish and then help her reach her goals. She will grow in self-confidence and personal strength as a result of your combined efforts.

Start talking with your child about her dreams and yours. Help her realize that we are never too young or too old to have dreams. Make it a regular family activity, maybe something you talk about during dinner or before bed every few weeks. Start keeping a record—maybe dream journals, one for her and one for you. Work on them together, sitting side-by-side and having fun sharing and writing down her dreams and goals and yours. Look for patterns or themes. Create a collage as a visual reminder of your ideas. Cut out pictures from magazines, print images off the computer, or make sketches. Study about your dreams together: read about them on the internet, check out books at the library, post pictures in your bedrooms or the kitchen, and identify role models and study their lives and the journeys that led to accomplishing their dreams.

Ask your child to think about what she would be willing to do to make a dream come true. What would she risk for it? What would she give up for it? What trade-offs would she make? Would she risk public embarrassment to perform in a play? Give up screen time to play soccer? These are critical conversations for you as a parent to start and keep going. They will help her visualize herself pursuing her dream and how doing so could change her life. Help her dream big and prepare to make those dreams truly transform her life for the better.

SPELLING LIST UNDER MY PILLOW: MAKING THE DREAM COME TRUE

"A dream doesn't become reality through magic: it takes sweat, determination and hard work."
Colin Powell

"…and three, two, one, action!" Goals move a dream from fantasy to action to accomplishment. Once your child has dreams that align with his values and priorities, and he can visualize himself living his dreams, it's time to start setting goals, those action steps that make dreams come true. In line with the size of the dream, it will cost time, money, and effort to actually pursue it and produce results.

There are several steps that can help your child stick to his goals and continue to make progress. The more clear and specific goals are, the more likely he is to have success. Encouraging him to share his dreams and goals with others will create in him a greater sense of responsibility to follow through.

Setting and following through on goals will change your child's life in ways that go far beyond the immediate successes. His resolve will grow, and he will develop willpower, self-discipline, and concentration. He will build a core sense of competency as he grows from dreaming, evaluating his dreams, choosing a dream to follow, visualizing himself being successful, and actually doing the hard work, step-by-step overcoming challenges and making his dream come true. This pattern will stick with him and become a lifelong strength.

Cal's Story

I was never a very good student, and I struggled in school. However, I had one teacher who believed in me. My fifth-grade teacher, Mrs. Bouck, made a significant difference in my life. Many of her methods were quirky, unconventional, and creatively made up to give me (maybe others, too) hope.

My most poignant memory was her motivational technique for helping me learn how to spell better. She motivated (perhaps bribed is a better word) us with candy. She gave weekly spelling tests and then rewarded us for our efforts. This simple reward was motivation for me to study my spelling words. We earned a candy bar if we got 100% on our spelling test for three consecutive weeks. Earning 100% for two weeks would get us a Tootsie Pop, while one test with 100% got us a piece of penny candy. Those who didn't get 100% on any of the tests received candy smarty pills.

She taught us that studying the spelling words right before going to bed was a great idea, and then told us to put the list under our pillow before falling off to sleep. She guaranteed that doing this simple study exercise would stimulate our brain to absorb, retain, and remember the spelling words. Using this unconventional approach, I started getting candy bars on a regular basis. Occasionally, I would mess up and only get a Tootsie Pop, but to my recollection I never got below that for the rest of fifth grade. Before adopting this unconventional study approach, I usually earned a piece of penny candy or smarty pills.

In reality, putting my spelling list under my pillow didn't help me at all to become a better speller, but perhaps Mrs. Bouck was on to something. Putting the list under my pillow made it more likely that I would study right before bed. When you make a habit of doing something at a specific time, you are more likely to continue doing it, and if you have an action associated with it, that makes the habit even stronger. Current research is clear that simple, immediate, and desirable rewards and recognition do motivate behavior change *and* that studying just prior to sleep can improve retention. She was conditioning me well!

As parents, we can help our children dream and set goals. We can teach them to work and study and can give them positive feedback. We can let them know that we are proud of their efforts and the baby steps they are taking towards their dreams. We can provide unconditional love so they are comfortable with open communication.

Just like Mrs. Bouck's "magical formula" helped a young boy who never thought he could get a 100% on a spelling test, we, too, can motivate our children to dream and reach their goals.

Parenting Strategy

Cal chose an adventure when he decided he wanted to earn the treats his teacher offered and accepted her idea for how to study to help him do just that. Help your child practice choosing his own adventures by picking dreams and age-appropriate action goals to take him there. Have a bit of fun with this; for example, ask your child if he would like to choose the adventure of making some popcorn, and ask him what steps he could take to complete this adventure. Then work on adventures further down the road in line with his age and interests: going to the movies on Saturday, taking a picnic to the park, reading a book by next week, graduating from high school, choosing his career, etc.

Children under the age of eight think more concretely, and their thinking slowly becomes more abstract as they mature. Age and maturity are important factors in the scope of dreams. Is your child ready to make commitments for a week, a month, a season, a school year? Eventually, as your child pursues small and concrete dreams, he will be prepared to choose lifelong career and lifestyle dreams.

Your child will have more success when he sets goals that are specific and a bit of a stretch, but not so difficult that they are unrealistic. Help him develop the habit of writing down his goals. This can be as simple as pictures and a few words for a younger child, all the way to a fully developed outline as your child matures. Be clear about each step, and encourage him to be thorough yet flexible enough to adapt as he gains experience.

Does your six-year-old want to play baseball at recess but is never picked? Help him set and work towards a goal to spend 10 minutes a day playing catch or practicing batting balls you pitch until he makes five hits. Gradually increase the time or number of balls he hits in your practices, and both of you will notice improvements as he gains experience and skill. Compliment him on his efforts, and mention any gains you see. Does your teen dream of making it big on the stage? Help him set meaningful goals to prepare for the school play tryouts by reading lines with you for a certain number of minutes or memorizing a certain number of lines per day. Have fun and enjoy the process along the way.

THE TEACHER SAID NO: CELEBRATE EFFORT AND PROGRESS

"Every great dream begins with a dreamer. Always remember, you have within you the strength, the patience, and the passion to reach for the stars to change the world."
Harriet Tubman

Help your child stay motivated to work on her goals by reviewing them with her regularly. Revisit her dreams. Help her keep her dream alive by reimagining herself living her dream. Is her dream becoming clearer and more compelling to her? Or is she discovering that it is fading and not as meaningful as it once was? Help her evaluate, move forward, or change accordingly.

Find ways to help your child enjoy the journey. Celebrate small steps along the way. Be proud of her as she travels along her chosen path. She needs your support while she is studying for her weekly spelling test, practicing her free throw shots in the backyard, or making a salad for dinner. She needs your encouragement and guidance in these small steps along the way just as much, if not more than, during the spelling bee, the big game, or the cook-off.

Celebrate her successes, of course, but most of all celebrate her efforts and ability to learn when she has missteps and setbacks. Help her see these as chances to reassess and adapt and as an inevitable part of stretching and growing. All of these small steps build foundational patterns for developing and pursuing her bigger-picture, longer-term life dreams and goals.

Our Story

Our son Peter was an exceptional student in math, science, and computers. Unfortunately, during his senior year, he suffered from a serious bout of mononucleosis, which led to him missing eight weeks of the first semester. At the time he was diagnosed, he was the top student in his A++ computer certification class. Unfortunately, due to the illness, he was sleeping 18 to 20 hours each day, and, when he was awake, he had no energy for homework.

The certification test was to be taken at the end of the first semester. Peter was confident he could pass it, so he approached his teacher and asked if he could take the test. He was told, "No! You have missed too much school and couldn't possibly pass it." I am sure that the teacher didn't believe in Peter and didn't want him pulling the class average down. Peter was persistent and eventually talked the teacher into giving him permission to take the test. When the test results came back, the teacher was surprised that Peter was the only student who passed the test and received his certification.

We were surprised with the teacher's reaction. Rather than being excited for Peter and what he accomplished, he let himself get embarrassed thinking that Peter showed him to be a bad teacher. After all, he was the only one of twenty students who passed the test, and he had missed most of the semester.

This experience demonstrates the importance of controlling our egos, working hard, overcoming discouragement, appreciating the challenge, and becoming stronger for the effort in achieving something many thought could not happen. Always remember the potential effect we can have on each other and the importance of supporting and encouraging one another when challenges arise. Doing so will help our children become more resilient and capable as they move through life.

Parenting Strategy

Critics and naysayers abound. Over the next day or two, listen for at least three examples of someone discouraging someone else unnecessarily. Share your findings with your child, and spend another day watching for naysayers in both your life and theirs. Now here comes the fun part, where being stubborn is a good thing! Challenge yourself and your child to stick with one thing you value that someone else discouraged you from doing. (This does not, of course, mean ignoring valid warnings of danger or doing things that put you in harm's way.) Talk about your experiment. What did your child learn? What did you learn? Would she like to try it again? Would you? What could you do next?

THE MIGHTY OAK AND THE LITTLE MAPLE: UNIQUE STRENGTHS AND CHALLENGES

"Everyone has his own specific vocation or mission in life.... Therein he cannot be replaced, nor can his life be repeated. Thus, everyone's task is as unique as is his specific opportunity to implement it."
Viktor Frankl

At a very early age, children start to dream of what they want to be when they grow up: a nurse, a rodeo clown, a teacher, a firefighter. These dreams usually shift and evolve as they gain experience in the world and an understanding of their unique strengths and challenges. An important job for you as a parent is to help your child explore and refine his dreams to suit his interests, talents, and values.

According to the legend of two trees[3], two seeds fell to the ground near one another. One seed was from a maple tree and the other seed came from an oak. The forest in which they lived was dense with fertile soil.

While they started out on the same day, the oak grew faster than the little maple, quickly becoming a beautiful tree. It was tall and benefited more from the sunshine and the rain. The little maple growing under the oak struggled.

---

3 Bryson, J. G. (1965). *One Hundred Dollars & A Horse: The Reminiscences of a Texas Country Doctor*. William Morrow & Company, New York, p. 52–53.

Years later, a craftsman came to the forest looking for a particular tree. He went from tree to tree, hitting their trunks with the back of his axe, and with his trained ear, listening to the pitch of the sound. The very size of the great oak precluded any interest from this particular craftsman.

The little maple was all bent and twisted and never became the beautiful tree that it could have been because it was growing under the mighty oak. When the craftsman saw the little maple, he dropped to his knees and listened carefully. As he tapped its trunk many times, he heard something he liked. He acted quickly and skillfully as he cut it down, carried it to his shop, and placed the pieces he wanted to use on a shelf.

He checked on the pieces frequently, anxiously awaiting the time when they would be ready to mill and he could move forward with his project. The day finally came, and the craftsman cut the pieces into thin slabs that he put in a press. Again, it took time for the pieces to be ready for the next step. When the time came, they were taken out of the press, bent, curved, and shaped into a beautiful violin. Lovingly, the craftsman placed it in his showcase with the other violins he had made.

Not long after, a famous violinist came into the shop looking for a violin that produced the perfect sound, which he found in the little maple. This violin had the tone that he had been seeking for years. So, the little maple, with all of its challenges and struggles to survive and thrive, became the creator of sounds with which the great master charmed and thrilled the world.

Parenting Strategy

Recognize your child's talents and resist the temptation to compare him to other children with different talents. Accept your child for who he is, appreciate his uniqueness, and praise his efforts. Teach him by your example to believe in himself; otherwise, you may both overlook a beautiful violin hidden within the little maple tree.

Whatever your child's strengths and challenges, he will thrive best if you help him learn to maintain a good balance in life. He will be more effective in pursuing long-term dreams as he learns to balance hard work with time for relaxation and fun. Maintaining a healthy lifestyle can be a powerful part of having the energy to stick with it and accomplish any big-picture dream. It's also a great place to practice setting and pursuing goals.

Even though you and your child may have very different life dreams, you may share some healthy lifestyle dreams. Would you like to wake up early and go for a run together, take a yoga class, fix and enjoy some healthy snacks, read a book, or just have more fun? Do you have common interests in serving in the community by preparing meals for the homeless, aiding refugees, or marching for social justice? Start small: set specific goals, review your experience, make adjustments as you plan your next step, and, most importantly of all, have fun together along the way.

Chapter 12

HARD WORK

*"Opportunity is missed by most people because it is dressed in
overalls and looks like work."*
Thomas Edison

GUNNYSACK FULL OF WOOL: THE PLEASURES OF HARD WORK

"I've always believed that if you put in the work, the results will follow."
Michael Jordan

Children today have incredible opportunities, undreamed of just a few short years ago. They have an amazing variety of nutritious foods, excellent health care, instant access to vast amounts of information, tremendous opportunities for education and recreation, and much more. Yet, all too often, today's children do not have one of the biggest advantages most children freely enjoyed throughout history: hard work.

Giving your child opportunities to learn the value and pleasure of hard work and experience a job well done will set her up for a lifetime of success, but let's face it, some jobs are a lot more pleasant than others. Help your child appreciate that each part of a task, including the tedious jobs of preparation and clean up, are all essential.

Hard work alone will not guarantee success, but, without a doubt, being unwilling or unable to work hard will keep most people from reaching their fullest potential. You should not promise your child that, by working hard, she can make all of her dreams and wishes come true. You can, however, promise her that if she works really, really hard, she can reach many—maybe even most—of her goals.

Many goals in life can only be achieved by people working together. As you teach your child to work, also teach her to work well with other people and be a good team member. Twitter, Facebook, Snapchat, internet gaming, and other technology can connect her with others in new and useful ways but can also take time away from personal, face-to-face contact. Too much communication through remote technology often leaves children feeling isolated and disconnected. Working with others—both digitally and in person—creates an increased sense of belonging and connectedness.

Daily routines and special events offer opportunities to work together. Involve your child in as much of the work as possible given her age and abilities. You can cook together, pack and unpack the car for a trip, repair the back fence, build a campfire, or plant, weed, and water a garden. There is nothing quite like sharing the warmth of a fire you built together, or eating freshly picked tomatoes you planted, tended, and watched grow and ripen all summer.

There was always plenty of work to do on Cal's family farms, and this helped him learn the value of hard work. As you read this story, think about ways to make work a part of your family's life.

Cal's Story

One of my memories as a young boy living in the small town of Afton, Wyoming was watching my grandfather shear his sheep.

222

I can still picture him grabbing a sheep by the wool, picking it up with two hands, and setting it down on its backside with all four legs sticking straight out. Holding the sheep in this position was the most efficient way to shear its head, belly, legs, and back. Of course, the sheep was not always a willing participant in this experience, so Grandpa had to hold it firmly with his left hand while using his right hand to cut away the wool with his electric shears.

When finished, Grandpa let the sheep get up and, before he sheared the next one, he gathered the wool into a bundle, tied it up with twine, and threw it to someone standing on a four-legged wooden frame holding a large gunnysack approximately eight feet long. The wool was thrown into this sack until it was full. Then it was sewn up with twine and set aside until all of the shearing was completed and all of the bags were full.

The first job I remember having was to climb to the top of the frame and jump into the gunnysack to stomp on the wool and compress it so more would fit into the bag. Even though I was only five or six years old and small for my age, I still thought I was the best wool stomper on the farm. Today, reality tells me that, because of my size, I couldn't have been a very effective stomper.

No longer believing that my efforts made much difference, I appreciate my grandfather even more. He let me keep stomping and helped me feel like an important member of the sheep-shearing team. I was so proud of my work and of contributing to the task at hand. I don't remember anything specific that Grandpa said to me, but he allowed me to work beside him, and I felt that my small contribution was appreciated. How did I know that? Because he loved me, he was patient with me, and he was kind to me.

Stomping the wool was a minor experience for me, yet it contributed mightily to who I am. Do we have gunnysacks where our children can stomp sheep's wool? If not, it might be good to find some.

Parenting Strategy

This might seem self-evident, but it is profoundly important: teach your child to value hard work by modeling it yourself. If she sees you give up on a project because it's hard, she will likely do the same. Are you willing to be a role model who sets a difficult goal and works hard to reach it? Try training for a race that would be a challenge for you, painting the bathroom, taking up kayaking, or learning to knit. Let your child see you struggle, tell her about your frustrations, show her how to take a break when you need it, then try again, stick with it, learn and improve. Let her hear you asking for help, inviting others to coach and encourage you, and sharing your successes and mistakes.

Our children need to learn the value of hard work, too, and as parents we must take responsibility in teaching this lesson. As we do, the day will come when they will understand that they are a valuable part of our family team. It might be easier, faster, and more efficient to do the work ourselves, but if we do that, they might get the message that we don't need their help. That message would be just the opposite of what we are attempting to instill in them. Besides helping them learn how to work, we are also helping them to feel loved and appreciated as valued members of the family team.

Perhaps your child is still young, full of energy, and willing to help, like Cal in the gunnysack. Yet, also like Cal, she may not be very efficient. So what? Remember, no one is very good at a task the first time they do it. Being bad at something is part of the learning process. Give her time to practice. Be patient and appreciative of her progress. Work alongside her and show her the way. Prepare her for the day she will be expected to be skillful and work on her own.

It does take time to help your child know that she is a valued member of the family team, but it is time well spent. How much time would it take to teach her how to clean up a mess, pull weeds, or paint a kitchen chair in the garage? Work together side-by-side, and tell her that her efforts are needed and appreciated. Tell others about her hard work and progress, especially when you know she can overhear you.

Challenge your child to take on projects that are difficult but possible. Encourage her to try a new hobby, take a class that might be hard for her, improve her batting technique, or try new foods. Encourage her to keep trying when things get tough. When she gets frustrated, teach her how to pace herself, take a break, relax, and then go back to work.

If you are not sure where to start, try something simple your child already loves and work up from there. For example, if your younger child loves chocolate chip cookies, start there. Get her involved in the planning. What time do we want the cookies to be ready? How long will it take to make them? So when should we start? Teach her where you keep the ingredients, how to get them out and put them away, how to measure, mix, and roll out the dough, and keep the kitchen tidy while you cook together. Make rinsing and washing as you go along a part of the routine. Show her how to set and watch the timer. Talk about how to prevent burns as you demonstrate how to take the cookie trays out of the oven, even when she is too little to do it herself. She will be learning and preparing for more responsibility. Sit down together to enjoy the warm, sweet, just-out-of-the-oven, scrumptious treat. Savor the moment and the rewards of hard work. Invite her to consider sharing some of the cookies. If she wants to share, let her choose with whom she would like to share them and go together to deliver the treats.

As your child grows older and more experienced, help her stretch her goals. If she knows how to bake cookies, she may be ready to prepare a whole special meal with you. Brainstorm and plan together what you want to have. Take an inventory of the necessary ingredients, look to see which ones you already have, and then shop for those you need. Figure out how long each dish will take to prepare and cook, determine the order in which you will work on them, and then calculate when to start in order to have all of the food ready when you want to eat. Divide up the chores: washing, chopping, measuring, mixing, sautéing, etc. Have fun working together: talk, laugh, and tell funny stories. This helps you connect and stay engaged and on task. Relax, enjoy being together, and be patient and gracious as you figure out together how to overcome setbacks and adjust plans when one step takes longer than you thought it would, the rice gets burned, or the avocado isn't ripe enough to use.

The same principles apply with all types of projects. Start with simple tasks, and increase the difficulty, complexity, and responsibility as your child grows. Whether the work is cooking, repairing an engine, remodeling the basement, learning to play baseball, or fixing a leaky sink, as you work with her and teach her, she will learn to be organized, stay on task, do the fun parts and also the boring ones, work to a deadline, and enjoy the satisfaction of accomplishment, all of which are important skills that will contribute to her growing resiliency.

UNCLE NEIL'S LARIAT: CREATIVE DETERMINATION

"It's hard to beat a person who never gives up."
Babe Ruth

Children with little experience working hard and successfully completing a project are often intimidated by the idea of starting a big task. They don't know where to start, how to measure progress, or how to overcome obstacles. Whatever your child's past experience, guide him, encourage him as his skill develops, and help him catch a vision of what he can accomplish through hard work.

As your child learns, his resiliency is strengthened by the feeling of confidence that comes from knowing how to work hard for what he wants. He will get that sweet feeling of accomplishment, begin to appreciate his own potential, and set his sights higher. He will become less afraid of failure, because he will learn from experience that setbacks are likely in any project, and he will know that he can make course corrections and bounce forward from challenges. He will be less likely to give up.

Growing confidence and determination impacts the kinds of friendships children are likely to make and keep. They are more likely to gravitate towards friends who also dream big, know how to work hard, and stick with their dreams. They are less likely to hang out long with people who shy away from meaningful goals, give up easily, or look to others to do the work for them.

Cal's Story

Uncle Neil was born and raised to be a rancher. He spent his entire life ranching in Afton, Wyoming. Like all successful ranchers, he worked hard and he worked long hours and taught his six children how to do the same. The boys were up early to milk the cows and feed the stock, and in the summer, they cut, baled, hauled, and stacked hay. The girls also had their chores, which kept them as busy as their brothers: weeding the garden, gathering eggs, hanging out the wash, and cooking the meals it took to keep them all fed.

Uncle Neil was a respected man, known in the community as friendly and helpful to others. He died at the age of 95, but this story occurred while he was living in a care center in Afton. He was always full of energy and was used to being outdoors all day, so even at an advanced age, sitting around all day with nothing to do was a form of torture to him. To make the day pass faster, he kept himself busy roaming the halls in his wheelchair and cheering up the other residents. The wheelchair was his only means of escaping the confinement of his room.

It was a sad day when the care center staff decided to eliminate his wheelchair meanderings. They devised a plan they were certain would contain Uncle Neil. Because he couldn't get around without the wheelchair, they moved it to the far corner of his room where they figured he couldn't get to it. But this old cowboy was not ready to be set out to pasture by being confined to his bed. He knew an old trick or two that would help him get the chair and cruise the hallways once again.

Everyone knows that a lariat (a rope used as a lasso) is a basic tool of a cowboy. This story would be pretty thrilling if Uncle Neil had smuggled a lariat into his room, but the real story is even more exciting. Like all good cowboys, Uncle Neil was an innovator who used what he had to get the job done. He disconnected his oxygen tubing, used it to make himself a lasso, and roped his wheelchair! Lickety-split, he pulled the wheelchair across the room and hopped in to ride the halls once again.

While I don't know what the staff thought of this talent, my imagination tells me their reaction was, "Oh, no, he's at it again!" His family loved it, and it became a cherished part of their history, a story to be shared over and over again with his grandchildren and great-grandchildren for years to come.

This simple little event demonstrated a lot of the skills Uncle Neil developed from early childhood and maintained throughout his 90-plus-year ranching career. He learned to work hard, have confidence in his abilities, be independent and resourceful, and take a problem-solving approach to life. His parents taught him the value of work, which he taught to his children, who are teaching it to their children and grandchildren one small step at a time.

The day our children are born, they start working towards their independence. Perhaps this year it is potty training; a few years from now, it might be driving a car. Before you know it, they are getting married and raising their own family. They need us as parents to teach them to work hard, one simple step at a time. This approach will never fail our children or us.

Parenting Strategy

As Uncle Neil so admirably demonstrated, a little creativity, work, and fun go really well together. Try combining fun with your child's regular chores. For example, try timing how fast he can feed the cat or empty the garbage. Of course, you need to teach him that you expect a job done correctly as well as quickly! Track his time every day for a week and see if he can beat his own time. Set up games such as "dirty laundry basketball" or competitive sibling speed-folding of clean clothes. (A small reward such as a free pass from doing the dishes makes the job even more fun.) Reward a job well done with extra relationship-building activities such as playing a favorite game or reading a story together. These special times are only limited by your imagination. Think outside the box. You will be surprised with your child's positive reactions.

Talk with your child about your dreams and visions, past and present. Tell him about obstacles you've faced and how you overcame them. Tell him about times you thought about giving up, and how you found the motivation to keep going. Tell him about your mistakes, and what you did to repair the damage and move forward. Encourage your child to talk with you about his hopes and plans, challenges, missteps, and next steps forward.

Tell stories to your child about family, friends, and others who have worked hard. Tell him how Uncle Ted built his cabin, then take them to see it and visit him, how Grandma went back to school after her kids were raised and started a new career, how your neighbor is learning to walk again after a serious accident. Read stories about famous people who became successful through hard work and overcoming obstacles, such as Michael Jordan, who was cut from his high school basketball team, or Steven Spielberg, who was rejected twice by the University of Southern California's School of Cinematic Arts. Conversations about others' journeys, as well as his own, will help your child develop insight into the value of hard work and build his sense of determination, resilient qualities he can use both now and in the future.

A FATHER'S HANDS: SPEAKING OF CHORES

"Success doesn't come from what you do occasionally. It comes from what you do consistently."
Anonymous

Getting children to do chores is a huge battle in many families. In the past, children's hard work was literally vital to the survival of most families. If children didn't get up and milk the cows, they didn't have milk for breakfast or butter for dinner, not to mention that the cows were standing there in the barn, mooing louder and louder as they waited to be milked. Dairy cows who aren't milked two or three times a day start to experience excruciating agony. They can quickly become ill and suffer an infection in the udder, known as mastitis, which can lead to death. Proper care of a farm family's animals has always been essential to their livelihood. Before the invention of labor-saving devices, there was simply more work to be done each day than mom and dad could possibly do without the kids. The pressure was on. The family needed children to do their chores the right way at the right time.

Most families today are not under that same kind of pressure for their children to do chores. As a parent, you could probably get all the chores done without help from your child. Changes in technology and culture have influenced how people work and how families are organized and spend their time.

In today's world, many people—both adults and children—view manual labor as work that is beneath them, and the implication is that those doing this work have a lower social status than those doing other kinds of work. Many children enjoy easy access to unending pleasures and excitement on their computers and smartphones. They resist working and even learning how to work.

It takes a lot of time and effort for you to teach your child how to do a job and follow through until she finishes. You may be tempted to give up and tell yourself, "It's just not worth the hassle." Please don't! The value of learning to work and enjoy the satisfaction of a job well done is as important as ever to developing lifelong resiliency. The payoff won't come immediately, but it will be worth it.

Cal's Story

Several years ago, I drove to Afton, Wyoming with my father, his wife, and my two sisters to attend the funeral of my uncle who had been a successful rancher his entire life. He was 95 years old when he passed away; he lived an honorable and productive life, and he was healthy for most of his life. This was a tribute to his hard work, which was a character trait of this great man. During the funeral, his son described his dad's hands as rough, gnarled, and callused by a lifetime of hard farm work.

While my cousin was speaking, I was sitting by another uncle who was in his 80s and has been a dairy farmer all his life. I glanced at his hands, and they were also chapped, cracked, and dry from milking thousands of cows over his lifetime. In addition to milking all those cows, his hands also mowed, hauled, and stacked thousands of tons of hay well before modern technology was available. They also planted and harvested thousands of acres of grain. I have always admired this uncle, and, as I looked at his hands a second time, I noticed those big hands tenderly holding the hand of his sweetheart of over 50 years.

Then I turned my head to the right and noticed the hands of my father, the cowboy barber, who left the farm in his 20s and over the next 65 years cut more than 100,000 heads of hair. I looked closely at his hands and saw that the hands roughened and callused by his days of working the farm had disappeared and had been replaced by hands conducive to cutting hair.

As I thought about these three men, whom I love and respect, I realized that there are many commonalities between each of them. Each of them was born and raised on farms, where they learned the importance of working until the job was done. They learned to appreciate their animals, treat them with care, and administer to their needs when they were sick or hurt. From their fathers they learned firmness, responsibility, gentleness, and kindness. From their mothers they learned to use their hands for service in their families and communities.

All three men depended on their hands to apply the lessons they learned from their parents. They used their hands to earn a living and support their families. Like their parents before them, these men used the skills they were taught to strengthen their children and give them hope for the future.

What a blessing to have hands that set an example of hard work, love, tenderness, service, and appreciation.

Parenting Strategy

Give your child regular responsibilities to:

1. Take care of her own belongings
2. Contribute to the well-being of the whole family

It's much easier to teach your child to work if you start when she is younger, but it's never too late. Whenever you start, start small and build on success. Your child will come to see herself as capable, competent, and reliable, key factors in developing the resiliency she will need in life. As she learns to pick up after herself and take responsibility for her own belongings, such as clothes, books, papers, toys, electronics, bed, closet, etc., she will gain a greater appreciation for the material possessions that make her life more pleasant and enjoyable.

By having her take on responsibility for chores that contribute to the family as a whole, she will feel more connected to and a part of the family. Some of the simplest tasks to start with are those involved in shared meal times, such as setting and clearing the table, helping with meal preparation, or doing the dishes. Even the smallest toddler can help. Research shows that having a sense of belonging is an important factor in developing resiliency. Combine that with feeling capable and competent, and you have a powerful blueprint for success.

Here are a few ideas to help ensure success:

1. Work alongside and teach your child new skills until she masters them. Instead of telling her, "Go clean your room," go with her, work together, and show her exactly what is expected. Set clear, age-appropriate standards for how to do the job and how to know when it is done.
2. Repeat this process until she demonstrates that she is capable and confident doing the chore on her own.
3. Increase the difficulty of the work and your standards in line with her age and growing abilities.
4. Talk about why each job is important, and how doing it will help her and the family.
5. After chores are done, reward her effort with time doing an activity of her choice together—set the amount of time and type of activity ahead of time. You do not need to spend a lot of money or even a lot of time. You will develop stronger bonds if the activities are interactive and rarely involve screen time. Your child will thrive from having your full attention while being playful and relaxing.
6. If, after doing everything as outlined, your child refuses to do a chore, establish consequences that are proportionate and as connected to the chore as possible. If, for example, your child doesn't put away her toy, phone, or papers by

the agreed-upon time, pick up the item and put it in a designated "collection" spot. When she wants the item, she can redeem it by putting away a reasonable number of other items of your choosing. If you assign your child to complete a chore before a particular activity, she will not be able to participate in that activity or another one until the chore is finished. Remain calm and firm in the face of protest. Be consistent, but not overly rigid. Use your own judgment and wisdom. Being either too rigid or too flexible will undermine cooperation. The important thing is consistency. Often parents forget to follow up because they get busy and distracted. Help your child learn that the choices she makes about chores have a real impact. Always offer her a way to repair a problem.

EIGHT HUNDRED PIECES: A SENSE OF OWNERSHIP AND PRIDE

"A lot of people want a shortcut. I find the best shortcut is the long way, which is basically two words: work hard."
Randy Pausch

Children feel a sense of ownership and pride when they work hard, resist the desire to quit, observe their progress, and celebrate when they complete a difficult task. Many people fantasize about winning the jackpot or achieving their goals with little effort, but, in reality, most successful people work very hard for their success. You can help your child experience this sense of pride and ownership by sweating together as a family on projects you believe in: prepping the soil and planting flowers to beautify your front walk, leveling the ground, digging post holes, and building a handicap ramp for your neighbor, or helping with a cleanup day at the park. Help your child stick to the task all the way to the end, and let him feel your pride in his contribution.

Hard work alone, however, is not enough. Your child also needs to know how to work smart and how to use the tools and techniques most likely to lead to success and needs to learn the value and importance of teamwork. Working without guidance and instruction is like trying to tighten a screw with a sledgehammer. You might work hard, but you are not likely to be very successful.

Our Story

We lived across the street from a beautiful home, and one day, while Anne was walking home from work, she thought, "If that house ever comes up for sale, maybe we should buy it." Later that evening, as we were sitting at the kitchen table eating dinner, she noticed a For Sale sign on that very house. She told Cal about her thought and asked if he wanted to go and check it out.

We went over to our neighbors, who invited us in to see the house. They took us on a tour, but before going through the house, our eyes were captivated by the beautiful chandelier that catches everyone's attention when they enter the front door. Its light is radiant, warm, and welcoming. Our neighbor told us the chandelier's history. It was purchased in the 1920s by her mother but was never hung until our neighbor bought this home in 1950. We loved the house and bought it that night!

The home was built in 1929. It has an upstairs that is only accessible by walking under the chandelier and up a winding staircase. Before moving in, we hired a contractor friend to restore the home to its original beauty and ambiance while also bringing it up to the current building code in order to make it safer for our family. The contractor mentioned that the chandelier could be a fire hazard and suggested that it be rewired. He knew our son Peter and thought he could do the work, so we hired him.

Peter enjoys that kind of work and was excited about this project. He started working immediately. We knew that when Peter takes on a project like this, he will do it right. He took the chandelier down and hung it from the ceiling in the garage. Before taking it apart, he took pictures from different angles so he would have a map for putting it back together, which definitely became a valuable resource.

Shortly after Peter started the project, we realized that we had a serious communication problem. We did not clearly explain what we meant by "rewiring" the chandelier. We thought he understood that we just wanted a simple electrical rewiring, but to his credit when he started working on it, he noticed that the crystals were dirty and the brass wire connecting them was tarnished and dull. So, with good intent, he carefully cut each crystal from the brass wire that had held them together for more than 80 years. He dismantled that beautiful chandelier into more than 800 pieces! When we saw what he had done, both of us felt like crying. Nevertheless, we held our tongues and encouraged him to finish the job.

This chandelier was an antique, and some of the parts he needed were no longer available, so he had to make them. One thing led to another; setback after setback occurred. There were crazy, unbelievable challenges. Over time, discouragement set in. The project floundered and lay untouched for months. Then, one day, an older sister and her husband volunteered to help him get it done as a surprise for us while we were gone on a weekend vacation. When we returned home, we were so excited to see that beautiful chandelier, restored to its glory, hanging back where it was always intended to be.

There are three very important resiliency skills in this story. First, accurately communicate the job expectations. Second, be sensitive to the time demand and provide help if a task becomes overwhelming. Third, profuse praise and encouragement are always nice.

Parenting strategy

1. Praise effort more than accomplishment.

Focus your praise on effort and improvement rather than accomplishment. Praise your child for trying something challenging and for sticking with the job. Encourage him to keep practicing and improving. Teach him to ask for and use the advice of experts. Imagine how having these experiences will help him develop the resiliency to tackle whatever challenges come his way.

Children naturally want to continue those actions that are positively reinforced by the adults around them. If they're praised for being naturally good at something, like maybe doing a cartwheel, but receive criticism when they work hard but fail at something, like going across the monkey bars, they learn to focus on doings things that are easy for them instead of learning that it can be rewarding to take the time to learn something that is a little more difficult.

Praise your child for all of his efforts, and take extra care to offer special praise when he works at those things that are hard for him.

2. Give specific praise.

"Good job" or "Good try" doesn't give your child the important information he needs about his actions. When you praise your child, be specific about what you saw and what you'd like him to continue doing.

"You made it three rungs farther across the monkey bars today than you did last time. You are getting stronger every time you try it" or "You worked so hard to research and write your book report! I thought it was great that you took notes while you were reading so you could remember the important information you wanted to include in your report" are much more helpful than a simple "Good job." Provide the extra support, direction, and encouragement needed.

3. Help when necessary, but never take over.

Sometimes your child really does need help, and when that happens, it's important to remember to help without taking over. Concentrate on guiding your child to find a solution or complete the task instead of doing it for him. Ask him questions or offer ideas. Show him and let him try for himself. Remember that letting him accomplish a task on his own, or even fail on his own, not only teaches him determination and hard work but also teaches him that you have confidence in him and believe he is capable of learning how to do things by himself.

Teach your child to recover and grow from failure. Again, model your own failures. (No, don't hide them!) Show him how you learned from experience and tried again, and maybe again. Share the little things, like plumbing disasters and cooking mistakes you've made. Show your child how you keep trying. When your child has a setback, help him learn to ask questions and try again.

4. Read books together.

Books can be a powerful tool for teaching your child life lessons. They give him an opportunity to relate to a character and to see different values in practice. There are several great books about teaching determination and hard work, including:

1. *The Most Magnificent Thing* by Ashley Spires
2. *Flight School* by Lita Judge
3. *Little One Step* by Simon James
4. *Thank You, Mr. Falker* by Patricia Polacco

THE 15-CENT JOB: LEARNING ALONG THE WAY

"Don't waste a good mistake....Learn from it."
Robert Kiyosaki

Nobody likes to see a child fail, but even this can be an important learning experience. Let your child make a mistake, and talk with her afterwards. Focus first on her hard work and the determination she showed while trying to solve the problem.

"You worked so hard to teach yourself a new song on the piano today. It was great that you spent the time to think about how the song sounds and to work to figure out the notes. Sometimes it's nice to take a break when we get frustrated and come back and try again a little later!"

Later, there will be time to come back and help her think about what went wrong and what she can learn from her experience.

Cal's Story

When I was 12 or 13, a friend and I decided to become big-time entrepreneurs by starting a lawn-mowing business. Our dreams were ambitious, and we envisioned making several hundred dollars each that summer. That would be the beginning of a burgeoning business that eventually would set us up for the future.

We had grandiose ideas, and we set about the task of recruiting customers. We didn't know anything about business plans, marketing, pricing, or public relations. All we knew is that we had access to a push lawn mower, a couple of rakes, and two pairs of hand clippers. So, we set out knocking on doors and asking the lady of the house if she would like to have her lawn mowed. (I say "lady" because, when I was a boy, women were usually the ones home.)

Our door approach was something that we hadn't thought much about and so whoever's turn it was would say whatever came into their mind. Most of the time, it went something like this: "Hi! (It always impressed them that two young boys were so polite.) My name is Calvert, and this is my friend Gene. We wonder if you would like us to mow your lawn?"

Usually they said, "No!" But, occasionally, someone asked how much we charged. That was a tricky question, because we had no experience pricing yards. We always approached potential customers with our equipment in sight, so they knew we were serious businessmen. This was before modernization took over the lawn-mowing business and everything was hauled in a truck. We had to walk to our jobs carrying and pushing the equipment. Frequently, we would negotiate a price, the woman would suggest we do her lawn for the agreed-upon price, and then she would think it over and decide if she wanted us to do it on a regular basis.

Our services were standard for the time and included mowing, raking, and trimming. We mowed with a push mower, raked with a real rake, and trimmed the border of the entire lawn, including around all the trees and shrubs, on our hands and knees using hand clippers. Depending on the size of the lawn, it would take anywhere from one to three hours, and we would earn $1.50 to $4.00. (See what I mean about no experience pricing a job?)

One day, a widow who lived down the street from me saw me pushing my lawn mower and called me over to ask how much I would charge to mow her lawn. It was a small lawn, and I figured that we could do it in 10 minutes. I knew she struggled for money and felt sorry for her, so impulsively I said, "15 cents!" She was excited, but my partner was not—he lacked the charity I felt. With some effort, I talked him into it. The 10 minutes I thought it would take us turned into more than two hours. She was picky and extremely hard to please. It didn't matter how much charity I had for this woman, we never mowed her lawn again. It's not that I didn't want to, but I took so much flak from my partner that I had to give him the entire 15 cents!

My lawn today is approximately the same size as the widow's lawn, but it costs me $20 to have it mowed, raked, and trimmed, and it only takes two guys 10 minutes to complete. (I learned my lesson though; I'm not picky!) Technology has made lawn mowing much more efficient, but certainly not less expensive!

Parenting Strategy

Cal knew how to care for a lawn and learned a lot from starting his own yard care service, but it was a big step without any guidance and with lots of mistakes to learn from! Although Cal's experience is pretty funny in hindsight, in many ways, it is also a sad story of missed opportunity. Cal's dad was a self-employed barber, and Cal could have learned a lot from his business experience in setting prices, recruiting and retaining customers, and working with partners.

Set your child up for success by giving her appropriate guidance and then let her make and learn from her own mistakes. Encourage her to work just beyond her current skill level. Pick one thing she already does well and think how she can take it just a bit farther. Does she clear her dishes but leave her napkin on the table? Help her take the next stretch. Does she start her homework but get distracted? Brainstorm together ways to keep on track: set a timer, reward herself with a two-minute break after twenty minutes of study, or stand up and stretch after every set of math problems. Be open to her ideas as well as your own, let her choose which to try first, and help her evaluate her experience.

Cheer her along as she figures out what works for her and what doesn't. Praise her effort and progress. Help her realize that what she is doing now is rewarding in itself and lays the foundation for resilient successes to come.

Chapter 13

SPIRITUALITY

"We can no more do without spirituality than we can do without food, shelter, or clothing."
Ernest Holmes

THE CHRISTMAS THAT CHANGED OUR LIVES: HOW DOES LOVE START?

"As soon as I saw you, I knew an adventure was going to happen."
Winnie-the-Pooh

Does your child seem disconnected, bored, or irritable? Are you worried about how much time he spends glued to his screens, playing video games, watching shows, or being caught up in the world of social media? Does he seem to lack a sense of purpose or drive? Is his life more consumed with digital scores and rewards, hashtags, snapchats, or tweets than face-to-face connections with other human beings, with nature, or even with the divine?

Developing your child's resiliency through spiritual growth can be a vital part of breaking free from these troubling patterns. Think of spirituality as the sense that we are all part of something bigger than ourselves and that our lives have meaning. People who see themselves as being spiritual in this sense may or may not belong to an organized religion. Many of us experience profound spiritual moments when life events prompt us to explore the meaning of birth, death, and the life that occurs in between.

When Anne's daughters were growing up, they had a guest from Germany in their home for the summer. Her name was Gabi, and she was 18 years old and doing an internship at Anne's father's company. One day, Anne's brother called to let her know that his wife had just safely delivered their third child, a little girl, and he invited Anne to come visit. Gabi quickly asked if she could come, too. Anne's brother agreed. On the way to the hospital, Gabi confided that, as an only child growing up in Germany, she had never held an infant before.

As Gabi sat in the hospital room, cradling that beautiful little baby, just a few hours old, tears began to flow down her cheeks. Surprised, she exclaimed, "I don't know why I'm crying, but I just am!" Sometimes deeply spiritual experiences take us by surprise and flood us with a powerful sense of wonder.

Cal's Story

Christmas arrived two days early in 1982 and was the best Christmas my family and I ever had. At about 10:30 that morning, I was in the garage working on some Christmas toys when Carol, my first wife, called me to the phone. Carol told me the call was from Ione Simpson, and I knew this could be a special call. I stopped what I was doing and hurried to the phone. (This was pre-cell phone days, so Carol was on the phone in the kitchen, and I answered the extension phone in the bedroom.) When I said "Hello," Ione asked one question: "Are you sitting down?" Those four words stimulated hope and excitement in both of us. Her next comment changed our family forever: "We have a little boy who was born yesterday. He is a beautiful little boy, and we wondered if you would like to adopt him."

Tears flowed freely down our cheeks, and in unison we replied, "Yes!" I believe Ione also shared a few tears with us. After nine years of hoping and praying and waiting, we were grateful that this day had finally come. We wanted this little boy more than anything in the world, and, even though we had never met him, we already loved him. We knew that he was an answer to our prayers and belonged in our family. For the next several minutes, Ione shared a little about our new son's history. We learned that he had been born the day before, on December 22nd. He was a little premature and small, so he would need to stay in the hospital for a week or so, but otherwise he was healthy.

We shared the happy news with our older son, who was 12. He had also waited a long time for a little brother and joined in our celebration of happiness. We changed our clothes and rushed to Primary Children's Hospital, where Ione took us to meet the newest member of our family. We all cried when we saw him sleeping in a small incubator with wires in his head, arms, and feet. He was so small and yet so perfect. He had just a few wisps of hair left on his head; most of it was shaved off so they could attach the wires that helped his doctors and nurses monitor him and keep him safe.

I walked over to look at his little face for the first time. He was lying on his stomach, sleeping, and then it happened, the most incredible experience—it felt as though his little spirit jumped out of his body and into my heart, with his little arms trying to wrap themselves around my neck to give me a hug. I thought this was his way of telling me he loved me and was glad to be in our family. At that moment, my love for him was cemented and has only grown stronger as he has grown older.

Reluctantly, we left the little guy to finish preparations for an extended family Christmas party being held at our home that evening. Driving home, we devised a surprise plan for telling everyone about the new addition to our family. We had invited Santa Claus to attend the party and deliver presents to the children. After all the presents were handed out, Santa delivered a special present to my mother.

The gift was a letter from our newest son, whom we named Peter. My mother opened it and read it out loud so we all could hear the "little guy" introduce himself to the family and express his gratitude for being a part of it. There was a P.S. at the end of the letter inviting his grandparents to visit him at the hospital.

By the time Mom finished reading his letter, there was not a dry eye in the room. Excitement prevailed, and happiness exuded from everyone present. As a family, we felt a calm assurance that together we could face whatever challenges lay ahead and that our experiences would strengthen the bond that already existed in our home. It's been 36 years since that phone call, and there have been ups and downs, as with every child, but our joy for having this little boy—now a man—in our family has never wavered.

Parenting Strategy

The birth of a baby, whether in your own family or someone else's, can be an amazing way to help your child deepen his sense of connection. It's a great time to talk about the nature of loving relationships. How does love start? What keeps it alive? Is it worth it? Most children love to hear stories of their own birth and how you came to love and care about them. Tell your child these stories over and over so that they sink deep into his sense of himself. Tell him stories about your own birth and the family you came from, your parents' births and their families. Research shows that children become more resilient when they know the stories of their family, the triumphs and the downfalls and the "how we got up from that." Feeling connected and part of something bigger than himself will help your child be better prepared to face his own challenges, both now and in the future.

ROBIN ON A WIRE: INTERCONNECTED

"There is really no natural limit to the practice of loving kindness in meditation or in one's life. It is an ongoing, ever-expanding realization of interconnectedness. It is also its embodiment. When you can love one tree or one flower or one dog or one place, or one person or yourself for one moment, you can find all people, all places, all suffering, all harmony in that one moment."
Jon Kabat-Zinn

Many spiritual traditions teach that all life is interconnected. Individuals, families, and formal and informal faith communities have diverse ways of honoring that connection. Some people relate most strongly to animals, whether household pets, baby lambs at a farm, or birds outside the window. Others connect with plants and enjoy filling their homes with potted plants, gardening, or stopping to smell the proverbial—or literal—roses. Some feel the interconnection most powerfully when they are having a wilderness experience in the woods or at a lake, river, or ocean.

Consider how you feel and understand your connection with the other forms of life with which we share our planet. Do you think about these interconnections when you choose what to eat, where to live, or how to use the world's natural resources?

Cal's Story

It was a lazy, hot summer day between my fifth and sixth grades. My friends and I were anxious to try the slingshots we had made using old bicycle inner tubes and forked branches. At first, we shot at inanimate objects, but we soon lost interest and decided to go bird hunting.

We were enjoying ourselves, pretending to be big-time hunters shooting imaginary game, until I saw a bird approximately 75 feet away, sitting on an electrical wire. Carefully, I picked up a rock, put it in my slingshot, took aim, and let it fly at the little robin. The rock hit it and knocked it off the wire. My friends started slapping me on the back, giving me a lot of kudos, and I felt like the mighty hunter I was pretending to be.

I hurried to the little robin. It was barely alive. I picked it up, and it died in my hands. Suddenly, the joy and fun of our little hunting adventure turned to guilt. I had just taken the life of a little bird that didn't deserve to die.

I didn't cry, because I was with my friends and thought that crying would have been a sign of weakness, and no 11-year-old boy wanted that. I controlled the tears, but inside I was shedding bucket loads. To this day (nearly 60 years later), I still remember the sorrow and pain I felt holding that dying little bird in my hands.

This mighty hunter kept his slingshot and continued playing but never shot at another living creature. Somehow, killing an innocent bird just for fun was no fun at all.

Parenting Strategy

Cal loves to tell his children and grandchildren about his experience with the robin and how it shaped his reverence for all living creatures. Examine your own life experiences and personal belief system. Have you ever had moments when you felt that you were part of something bigger than yourself? Ever gazed up into the night sky and wondered about your place in the immensity of space? Ever thought about the meaning of life? Such experiences are part of your own spiritual journey.

Now, start sharing your journey, whatever it has been, with your child. Tell her about how you think through the big questions of life and what gives it meaning and purpose for you. You do not have to have all the answers, just a willingness to explore and learn together.

Experience the beauty of life together with your child in big and little ways. Stand on a mountain and watch the sun rise; wade in a creek on a summer day; chart the moon as it waxes and wanes over the course of a month. Recently, we had the opportunity to drive to Rexburg, Idaho and witness a total solar eclipse together. It was incredible beyond words to watch as the earth, moon, and sun aligned perfectly, just as predicted. We watched in awe as we felt the light and temperature slowly drop as the sun was 80%, 90%, 98% obscured. At the moment of totality, we witnessed continuing wonders as the sun's corona shimmered around the moon, the birds fell silent, as did the cows and other animals, and the horizon glowed with a 360° sunset. When the sun gleamed out from behind the moon, for an instant the sparkling "diamond ring" flashed before our astonished eyes. The bond of sharing that experience with each other and the unknown strangers gathered in the same field and the millions of others across the United States will stay with us forever.

One-third of the world's population cannot see the stars at night, and 80% of Americans cannot see the Milky Way anymore. If you live where you can't see the stars, it is worth the effort to go to where you can. Allan Sandage, renowned astronomer, spent his life studying the stars and unraveling the mysteries of the universe. His appreciation for its beauty and constancy led him to embrace a belief in a creator. Whatever your beliefs, whether you travel long distances or sit together in your own backyard, savor your experiences of beauty with your child. These moments provide a much-needed respite from the busy world.

Help your child understand the interconnection of all life. Give her opportunities to provide life-giving care to your family dog, a goldfish, or even a plant. Talk about how all of us depend on others to meet our needs. Create a poster that shows your interconnections with the plants and animals that provide your food and clothing. Take a nature walk in the city or out in the wild. Turn over rocks, watch as the insects scurry away, and talk about their vital roles in the life cycle. Point out bird nests, animal burrows, beehives, and spider webs. Teach your child to protect and maintain natural habitats and honor life in all its forms.

Bob and Dave Are Friends: Facing Life and Death Together

"Walking with a friend in the dark is better than walking alone in the light."
Helen Keller

Years ago, Anne was a social worker at an agency that served low-income seniors. Most of her clients were in their 80s and 90s; one was 104! Not surprisingly, quite a few of her clients passed away, and Anne's friends asked if this was depressing to her. After giving it some thought, Anne realized that the value and joy of knowing these amazing people far outweighed the pain of their loss. And so it is with all relationships. We never know how much time we will have with someone we love and care about, and building connection is always worth the effort. Developing a deeper sense of connection with others and recognizing that all life is fleeting and will come to an end are important parts of spiritual resilience.

Anne's story

It all began with two teenage boys, Bob and Dave, my dad, growing up in the late 1930s and early '40s. Bob was born with a cleft palate, which, although repaired to the extent possible at the time, still had some obvious impacts on his appearance and speech. Not everyone at school looked beyond these to get to know Bob's talents, strengths, and potential. This was not the case with Dave, who accepted him for who he was and was proud to call him his friend.

Their friendship lasted over 50 years. As the boys became men, their appreciation, respect, and admiration for each other continued to grow. Together, they went through war, weddings, schooling, graduations, births, relocations, sickness, and finally death. Both boys grew up to be intelligent men who graduated from college with professional degrees and were successful in their respective careers. They both married and raised large families, with all of the associated ups and downs and trials.

In his early 60s, my dad was diagnosed with Alzheimer's disease, and their friendship grew even stronger. After Dad's diagnosis, Bob visited his friend every week and spent precious time with him. At first, they went for a jog together and talked as they ran, then a jog became a long walk. Eventually, the walks became shorter, walking turned to shuffling, Bob started to push Dad in a wheelchair, and then he simply sat by his side. Most important of all, Bob continued his visits every week without fail until the very end.

It has been said that "Life is better with friends." Such is the case for Bob and Dave.

Parenting Strategy

Friendship is one of many ways your child can feel connected with others. The relationship between true friends is a remarkable experience that pays huge dividends. Help your child understand what a true friend is, the work it takes to maintain such a friendship, and the value it can bring into his life. Help him realize that real friends are there for each other when things go well and when life takes a turn for the worse.

Like Dave, someday each of us will die. Sometimes we want to shield our children from this hard truth. Instead, help your child see that facing life and death and everything in between together with those we love and care about is what brings us some of the great joys this life has to give.

Start with little things, like giving a book or other small gift to someone who is sick or injured. Take your child with you and spend a few minutes with an elderly neighbor or relative, listening to their stories, asking questions, or fixing a meal. Talk about the seasons of life and help her understand that every living thing will grow old and die. Share whatever beliefs, ideas, or even questions you have about what happens after we die. Share what other people around the world believe. You don't have to be an expert; just be curious by studying it together on the internet or at the library and by asking others. Encourage your child to ask questions, then answer them as honestly as you can. You will be helping him share with you and the rest of humanity the wonderful journey of discovery about the meaning and value of life. Bon voyage!

SNOWSTORM BLESSINGS: HELPING THOSE YOU CAN REACH

"The best way to find yourself is to lose yourself in the service of others."
Mahatma Gandhi

Life today is busy, busy, busy. Spirituality is about feeling a sense of connection that is above and beyond our daily lives. Simple spiritual practices are an important way to create a break from the endless pressures and to-do lists of life. Daily, weekly, and seasonal traditions can help to refresh you. Some people practice a few moments of gratitude daily. Others attend formal religious meetings or give service on a regular weekly basis. Some find joy in returning to a favorite quiet spot in the desert or mountains each year.

In addition to regular, planned practices, other opportunities come when least expected. This is what happened one winter day when Mother Nature declared that life would not go on as usual.

Our Story

In January 2016, an enormous snowstorm hit the Washington, D.C. area, dropping nearly three feet of snow. The weatherman predicted the storm, but it was much more intense than expected. As the storm subsided, people began to venture out into the quiet streets where the deep white drifts covered everything and dampened all sounds. Our son Paul and his two teenage sons, Edwin and Matthew, went outside to clear their driveway and then stayed out with several other neighbors to help clear the snow for those who couldn't do it for themselves.-

School was canceled the next day, so the boys went out and helped more neighbors. By the afternoon, many of the major roads had been cleared, so Paul and his sons drove over to help some friends living outside their immediate neighborhood. I don't know how motivated the boys were by then, but they went with their dad and cleared another sidewalk and driveway.

When the job was done, Paul went inside to talk with his friend. Unbeknownst to him, Eddie had started shoveling yet another sidewalk. Paul stepped back out, and at first he was frustrated when he realized what Eddie had started. It was late, he was tired, and it was time to go home. However, he and Matthew pitched in, and together they cleared the sidewalk.

The following week, they learned that an older couple lived in the last house and had been out of town visiting their daughter who was undergoing cancer treatment. They were exhausted as they drove home, emotionally and spiritually drained. They had heard about the snowstorm, and knowing that they would have to shovel their sidewalks and driveway when they got home only added to their burdens. When they arrived home and saw that some "Good Samaritan" had cleared away all of their snow, their exhaustion turned into exhilaration and gratitude.

The few minutes Paul and his sons spent doing a kind deed benefited them all. The elderly couple felt loved and supported, even by strangers. Paul and his boys shared the sweet feeling that comes from kindness and generosity. They learned the value of serving others and giving freely of themselves. Now, as they continue giving service, their spiritual resiliency is growing and will bless and benefit them throughout their lives.

Parenting Strategy

Within every challenge is an opportunity. Who knew as the storm gathered and the flakes began to fall that here was an opportunity for building community and spiritual growth? Rather than struggling alone, family, neighbors, friends, and strangers reached out, shared the struggle, and made connections. Help your child look beyond his own troubles and responsibilities, and he will gain a new perspective and understanding of the value of giving and receiving kindness, service, gratitude, and connection.

Help your child feel connected to others in many ways. When you hear of another person's challenges or pain—in your neighborhood, on the news, close at hand, or far away—make a habit of saying out loud, "I'm sending good thoughts to _____." Remember them in your family prayers if prayer is part of your spiritual practice.

Then take it a step further and think of something tangible you can do to help. For example, when someone nearby is having a hard time, go with your child and take over dinner or flowers, make a card, mow a lawn, or shovel snow. For troubles far away, find ways to help through one of the many fine religious and service organizations that are making a difference. Share their mission on Facebook or post a photo on Instagram. Make a pledge, run a marathon, or raise money. When you are unable to help those who are far away, being aware of their pain can motivate you to help those you can reach.

OPERATION BREAD: WE ARE NOT ALONE

"If you light a lamp for somebody, it will also brighten your road."
Buddha

Spiritual practices offer a chance to step away from our daily routines, whether watching a sunrise, lighting candles, singing in a choir, or summiting a mountain. Repeating such experiences helps create an ongoing pattern of renewal and an awareness of life beyond the pressures of the day-to-day that can be profoundly satisfying.

Organized religion has played a huge part in the human experience and has impacted history and culture in innumerable ways. Educate yourself and your child about this complex and intriguing history. This group of people believes this, this other group believes this, I believe this, or I'm not sure what I believe. These are some of the controversies, some of the strengths, here is how things have changed over time, etc.

Visit different places of worship, attend different cultural and religious events, and study the history, beliefs, and practices of different religions and spiritual pathways. Share your thoughts and feelings. If there are practices or beliefs that resonate with you, you can adopt them as a part of your family culture whether or not you are already affiliated with an organized religion or are drawn to join an organization. For example, certain faiths have rituals for grieving; for celebrating the changes of the season, births, deaths, and other milestones in life; for giving service; and for expressing gratitude and hope. You can draw inspiration from these traditions, adapt them to fit you, and add what feels right to your own life.

Cal's Story

My grandson Calvert and I went to Mali, Africa to visit my son, who was there for two years as the military attaché to the US Embassy. We all really looked forward to this trip, because whenever the three of us go on an adventure, we can always count on having a fun, exciting, and crazy time. We never know what is coming next. Our attitude towards planning is simple: we always seem to fly by the seat of our pants.

On this trip, we tried something a little different. In the evenings, instead of seeking out the usual forms of vacation entertainment, we devised a plan we named "Operation Bread." We decided to buy and then give away as much bread as we could purchase with 6,000 CFA (approximately 10 USD).

The first night, we were able to buy 20 regular loaves of bread, plus 5 loaves known as "soup bowl loaf" and one loaf of shortbread cake. We spent an hour or so driving around Bamako, the capital city, giving loaves of bread to any women we saw with small children, pregnant women, little children begging, and any handicapped people.

The next night, we once again set out to share our bread. After buying the bread, we stopped at another store and bought some fruit juice for ourselves. We purchased a liter of juice for each of us. I drank about one-third of mine before we stopped to offer bread to two young girls, who were about 11 or 12 years old. They were excited by the gift, and then asked us for a drink.

My son, always known for his quick wit, reached over and kindly gave my drink to the girls. Their smiles grew bigger, their eyes were brighter, and it was worth losing my orange juice.

We saw five young boys and gave them a loaf of bread. As we turned to leave, we were upset to see the biggest boy take the loaf. We watched for a few minutes thinking that he was stealing it for himself, but we were wrong. He took the loaf and carefully divided it into pieces, giving a piece to each boy. All of the boys waited patiently until each one had a piece. When the biggest boy was done, he looked around, then took the bread he had given to one of the smaller boys, measured it against the one he had kept for himself, broke off some of his own piece and gave it, along with the original piece, back to the smaller boy. Wow! We were humbled by the beautiful lesson in kindness and caring taught with simple power by hungry boys.

As we were coming to the end of our adventure, we offered bread to two people on the side of the road: a woman who seemed to have some kind of severe mental health issue and a man confined to a wheelchair. As Calvert got out of the car, walked over to the man, and gave him some bread, he paused and spent the next 10 minutes or so just talking, creating a little friendship with the man.

What great delight we enjoyed together on this vacation. What joy we felt sharing our bounty and ourselves with others, doing something as simple as passing out bread to strangers in need, and pausing to speak, smile, and connect.

Parenting Strategy

Giving a gift with no thought of return, giving service to those who cannot repay the favor, and improving the world around us for the benefit of all are acts that help us remember that we are connected to something bigger than our own personal self.

With a bit of intention and commitment, it is not that hard to find and follow through on opportunities to share such experiences with your child. Look in your local newspaper or online forums for service opportunities. Keep your ears open for stories of people in need, homeless shelter projects, refugee services, pet adoption fairs, or community gardens. The opportunities are all around.

Generally, giving time and energy is more personal and connecting than giving money. Make a difference together. Invite your child to work alongside you, maybe invite their friends to come along, too, and make it a memorable day. Finish the day off with a picnic at the park or stop for an ice-cream cone.

Actively participating and contributing to the greater good is a life-affirming way of strengthening a sense of connection to something of value beyond daily life. You and your child will build resiliency as you make spiritual practices a regular part of your family life. You both will come to know that you have much to give and much to receive. You will realize at a deep level that you are not alone. All can participate, each in his or her own way. All have something to contribute: the young, the old, the strong, and the weak. We are all in this together!

Chapter 14

CONCLUSION

"All endings are inexorably tied to new beginnings. That's the nature of the journey. It continues to unfold. It builds on itself. It can't help itself from doing that. Cherish the moments, all of them. You have seen and felt much in life so far. But still, the best is yet to come."
Melody Beattie

There Is No End

This is the best part of all—there is no conclusion. Parenting is the perfect never-ending story, an amazing Choose Your Own Adventure series with endless possibilities. The story goes on; growth and change continue.

Like most parents, you probably started this book with a desire to help your child overcome her current problems, mature, and succeed in life. Again, like most parents, as you helped her, you probably ended up growing more resilient and resourceful right along with your child; you cannot teach what you do not live yourself.

You have learned to lead the way, gently nudging, nurturing, and protecting as needed. It's been an exciting journey as you and your child have built valuable resiliency skills that will last a lifetime. No matter where you are now, the marvelous (though sometimes crazy) journey will continue on, through all the ups and downs of life.

RESILIENCY IN ACTION

Resiliency, as we've been learning, is the ability to get knocked down by life's challenges, whatever they are, then struggle and learn from the process and bounce forward. Children today face a wide range of challenges, both the ones that children have always faced and many new and disturbing ones as well, such as online bullying, increased exposure to violence, and easy access to sexually explicit material, to name only a few.

Busy parents are stretched thin as they try to help their children do the best they can. Many parents run themselves ragged, chasing solutions for each new problem individually, whether it's managing cell phones and screen time, disrespect of authority, sibling rivalry, or any of the other problems families face.

In the pages of this book, we have shown you a better, more effective way. Through stories and practical strategies, we have explored how to help your child develop core life skills research identifies as essential to developing the resiliency he will need to overcome his challenges, both now and in the future.

COME BACK AGAIN

We suggest you come back often, review the steps to Setting Successful Goals, and re-read the stories and strategies. Every time you do, you will discover something new. Your child will be growing older and facing new challenges. It is difficult to stop, really listen, and respond effectively to your 10-year-old child when he wants to go play before doing his chores (see Chapter 12: Hard Work, A Father's Hands), and even harder when your 16-year-old wants to go to an unsupervised party (see Chapter 9: Values, On Belay). Helping your child learn to forgive her brother for eating her piece of cake or snatching his toy when they are both young is different than guiding your teenager to find peace after being bullied at school or publicly humiliated online (see Chapter 4: Forgiveness, Betrayal).

SCARY, BUT WORTH IT: THE PARENTING SWEET SPOT

It can be nerve-racking to let our children move forward in life. As adults, it is only too easy to see how quickly things can go wrong. Yet, we also know that if we never let them forge ahead, we are sending the message that we don't have confidence in them, and they will never gain the experience of trying, even making mistakes and finding their way back.

We continue to train and encourage them, constantly trying to find that parenting sweet spot between too much protection and too much risk. As scary as it can be to take calculated risks and let your child move forward, the rewards are tremendous as we see our children mature and develop (see Chapter 5: Self-Worth, A Mother's Belief).

Most of us as parents struggle over and over again to find that spot in each new phase of our child's development. Likely you've found—and maybe even lost—that spot many times as you've read this book, made changes in your parenting, and helped your child gain greater resiliency skills. This is how all of us grow, parents and children alike.

STORY TIME TRADITIONS

We love sharing our stories with you and hope you have enjoyed them as well. Everyone, including you, has stories to share. Storytelling has always played a big part in passing on wisdom from one generation to the next. We hope you are taking us up on our suggestion to tell your child stories from your own life, as well as some from ours (see Chapter 7: Family Traditions, Sitting at Grandma's Feet). Remember, your child will benefit from hearing about your successes and accomplishments, and she will learn even more from hearing about your troubles and mistakes and how you overcame them or how you are still working on them.

Telling your child stories about your life and what you have learned along the way is a powerful way of passing along your insights and personal values (see Chapter 8: Wisdom, Mrs. Wiggs). The stories we tell ourselves about our life experiences, how we interpret them, and the meaning we give to them may be more important than the actual experiences themselves.

Imagine that you are telling your child a story about going for a walk with me. While we were on the walk, I suddenly pushed you. What is the story you will tell? Will you conclude that I am just a mean person who can't be trusted? Will you tell your child that you were surprised, but decided to check it out and find out why I pushed you? Maybe you discovered that I tripped or that someone else bumped me.

Sharing stories is an effective way to nurture your child's resiliency. When you share stories about your life experiences, how you reacted, and what you learned, you give your child access to valuable life skills you have spent years cultivating, your personal wisdom, values, problem-solving skills, and so much more.

You don't need to be perfect to be a wonderful parent. None of us are. As you share stories with your child, he will likely start to tell you stories about his life as well. If you listen to him, you will learn more about him and draw closer together. You will be building a powerful tradition that strengthens your family's resiliency.

We want to be part of your continuing journey. We hope you will write to us, post on our website, include us in your discoveries, and send us your questions. You may want help implementing the inspiration and strategies found here. You may feel confused or want to talk over your progress. You may be excited and have stories to share with us or discouraged and need encouragement and support. If you contact us, we will answer. We continually update our website, so you will always find new resources there to help. If you have a question or topic you would like us to address, please let us know.

www.ResilientChild.com

Appendix

Setting Successful Goals Worksheet

Choose a comfortable place to sit with a hard copy of this worksheet and a pen or pencil, or your laptop or tablet. Take a couple of relaxing breaths and focus on the part of you that wants to grow or change. Think about a big picture change you would like to see.

A big picture change I would like to see is:

1. Small goals in the desired direction (Be sure that these are goals for the person with the dream. Usually that will be you!):

a.

b.

c.

d.

e.

2. Benefits. Ask the part of you that wants to make a change, "What would be the benefits of the growth or change I have in mind?" Write down all the benefits you can think of, read over your list, and rewrite any that are stated as negatives, making sure all benefits are stated in the positive.

a.

b.

c.

d.

e.

3. "BUTS." Move to another place to sit, take a couple more relaxing breaths, and focus on the part of you that says, "Yes, that sounds nice, BUT…" Write down everything that comes to your mind.

a.

b.

c.

d.

e.

4. Review your list and include an emotion to go with each of your thoughts. Search deep to find and label your emotions. There is always at least one emotion connected with each of these powerful "BUTS."

a.

b.

c.

d.

e.

5. Go back, read over your list of benefits, and pick the three that stand out, that mean the most to you personally. Put a little check mark by them. Then look over your list of "BUTS," and pick the three that are the most significant for you right now. Put a little check mark by them.

6. Write out the following script, filling in the first three blanks with the "BUTS" you selected, and the last three blanks with the benefits:

Even though _____

_____;

Even though _____

_____;

Even though _____

_____;

There is a part of me that wants and believes that I/we can _____

_____

_____ ;

There is a part of me that wants and believes that I/we can _____

_____

_____ ;

There is a part of me that wants and believes that I/we can _____

_____

_____ .

7. Read your script out loud. When you have finished, ask yourself this question, "How am I beginning to feel?" Make note of your answer and how you are beginning to feel in this moment. Pay attention to the intensity of your emotions, where you are experiencing sensations in your body, the type and intensity of these sensations, and what they might be trying to tell you.

Now you are ready for action!
Pick one goal and get started.

Repeat this process regularly as you work on stretching and reaching towards your goals for change and growth. Fine-tune your script as you make progress or when you run into new or unexpected challenges.

Effective Communication Worksheet

The topic I want to discuss is …

Check to make sure your topic is your underlying concern, not a solution you have already decided on . For example, "I want to talk about how we do laundry" is a topic, while "I want you to put away your clean clothes" is a solution. Rewrite if necessary.

Prepare yourself by completing the following:

1. How do you aspire to be in the conversation? Write down some words that describe how you would like to be during this conversation. For example, you might want to stay calm, be patient, be curious, be clear, or be kind.

    a. During the conversation, I want to be…

    b. Choose one word from your list that seems the most important for this situation and write it in large letters here:

    c. Now think of a time you had this quality, even a little bit.
    d. Recall the experience as vividly as possible. Remember how you felt, both physically and emotionally, and recapture that experience in your imagination as

strongly as you can. Answering these questions might help you.

    i. Where were you?

    ii. Were you inside or outside?

    iii. What did the place look like?

    iv. What time of day was it? Time of year?

    v. What was the weather like?

    vi. Were you sitting or standing or walking?

    vii. How did the chair or beach or bench feel as you sat or walked?

    viii. What were you wearing?

    ix. Were there any noticeable smells?

e. As you recall your experience, you are replaying a mini-movie of success. Give your experience a name, like the title of a movie.

2. What do you hope to accomplish in your conversation?

a. Check the line that best describes your purpose:

    i. Give information

    ii. Share thoughts and feelings

    iii. Solve a problem

    iv. Offer support or encouragement

    v. Strengthen relationship

    vi. Other

b. Keep your purpose in front of you throughout the conversation and remind yourself often what you are trying to accomplish and how you aspire to be regardless of how your child chooses to be.

3. Are you ready to put it all together? Here are the next steps for success.

    a. Turn off your cell phone. (Yes, really! This sends the message that your child is important enough to have your full attention.) Invite your child to talk with you and let her know you care.

    b. Tell your child what you would like to discuss. If solving a problem or making a decision is part of what you want to accomplish, explain that you are going to take those off the table until you both have had a chance to speak and be heard.

    c. Invite your child to go first and tell you her thoughts, feelings, and desires about the topic. Resist the urge to cut her off or start talking about how you see the situation.

    d. Listen with great empathy. See the world through her eyes. What she is feeling and thinking makes sense to her. Look at the world from her perspective, and then speak her reality out loud, especially when it is different from your own.

    e. Be curious: ask clarifying questions, recap often and respectfully, and stay focused on her. She needs to feel that you are sincere and caring, not just parroting her words back to her. Let her know that all of her thoughts, feelings, and desires are OK. Make it safe for her to be honest and open with you, even when what she is thinking, feeling, or wanting is uncomfortable or not what you were hoping for.

    f. Keep in mind what you want to accomplish and how you aspire to be in this conversation regardless of how she chooses to be.

    g. When you think she is finished, ask her if there is anything else she would like to say about this topic.

h. After she says that she has nothing more to add, start to speak with clarity about your own thoughts, feelings, and desires.

i. After you reveal your thoughts, feelings and desires, she may have something more to say, so take turns, going back and forth as long as needed to get meaningful understanding. Remember that understanding does not mean agreeing.

j. If you are looking for solutions or making a decision, now is the time to get some ideas out on the table.

   i. Ask your child for her ideas about possible solutions or decisions. Ask her to explain how her ideas honor and respect her concerns and desires as well as yours.

   ii. Present a few ideas of your own, along with your explanation of how you think they take into account her thoughts, feelings, and desires as well as your own.

   iii. As the parent, it is always your responsibility to make final decisions, yet consider your child's input as much as you can. Adapt and allow her more influence as she matures.

   iv. Make your decision and discuss it with her.

k. Whatever the purpose of the conversation, always end with a sincere expression of respect, caring, or appreciation.

EMOTIONAL GROUNDING WORKSHEET

Practice emotional grounding exercises regularly when you are calm so that they become automatic and you can use them easily even in the heat of a distressing moment. Take a 20-minute break once anyone in the family feels emotionally flooded. During the break, parents and children alike need to spend the time doing emotional grounding. Please model grounding, even if you think you don't need it. It is worth the time and will dramatically change the way your family gets along.

- **Come to Your Senses.** This technique uses your basic senses to bring you into the present moment.

  1. Begin with vision. Look around you. Without making any judgments, such as I like or don't like, name five things you can see. For example, "I see two red pillows, a clock, three windows, a chair, and a picture on the wall."
  2. Move on to five things you can hear. "I hear the air conditioner, a car, the clock ticking, birds, and the wind in the trees."
  3. Next, touch. "I can feel the pen in my hand, the tag of my shirt, the chair I'm sitting on, my feet in my shoes, and the pillow I'm leaning against."
  4. These three senses can be done anywhere, anytime, without anyone even knowing you are doing them. Depending on where you are, you can also use taste and smell.
  5. If you get through all of the senses and still feel distressed, go through them again naming four things, then three, two, and one.
  6. If you are still distressed, start over with five and keep going until you feel a sense of calm.

- **7/11 Breathing.** While you are breathing and counting, you are relaxing your body and taking a mini-vacation from thinking. No one can think about their troubles and count at the same time!

  1. Breathe in, and while you breathe in, count to seven in your head (slowly like you are counting for hide and seek, but silently in your head so you can also breathe).
  2. Pause for a moment when you get to seven.
  3. Then slowly breathe out, counting to eleven as you do. (The long out breath sends the message to your mind and body that you are safe and can relax, like a deep, long sigh when you sit down after a long day.)

- **Play some mental games.**

  1. Try reading backwards.
  2. Make lists of your favorite foods, bands, or cars.
  3. Find pictures of places you would like to visit.
  4. Count how many animals you can think of that start with the letter of your choice.

- **Do something active.** (But not aggressive, as being aggressive only keeps the stress chemicals going.)

  1. Go for a walk.
  2. Take a bike ride.
  3. Shoot a basketball.
  4. Do some yoga stretches.

- **Try something soothing.**

  1. Put a warm washcloth on your face.
  2. Splash your hands in cool water.
  3. Take a bath.
  4. Massage your face and neck.
  5. Read a book.
  6. Listen to soothing music.

Once you are comfortable with your emotional grounding exercises, follow a clear plan for managing strong emotions.

1. Recognize when you or your child is feeling under attack.
2. Take a break to let emotions cool and allow rational thought and good verbal skills to come back online.
3. During your break, use emotional grounding techniques.
4. After your grounding break, always go back and have the conversation you were going to have, bringing your best self to the table, as outlined in Tool #2: Effective Communication. This demonstrates your integrity and commitment and will strengthen your relationship and build family resiliency.

Bonus stories and strategies
available at

WWW.RESILIENTCHILD.COM

CPSIA information can be obtained
at www.ICGtesting.com
Printed in the USA
FFHW011020190719
53666753-59338FF